CAMBRIDGE
UNIVERSITY PRESS

Combined and Co-ordinated Sciences

for Cambridge IGCSE™

PHYSICS WORKBOOK

Sheila Tarpey, David Sang & Darrell Hamilton

CAMBRIDGE
UNIVERSITY PRESS

Shaftesbury Road, Cambridge CB2 8EA, United Kingdom

One Liberty Plaza, 20th Floor, New York, NY 10006, USA

477 Williamstown Road, Port Melbourne, VIC 3207, Australia

314–321, 3rd Floor, Plot 3, Splendor Forum, Jasola District Centre, New Delhi – 110025, India

103 Penang Road, #05–06/07, Visioncrest Commercial, Singapore 238467

Cambridge University Press is part of the University of Cambridge.

It furthers the University's mission by disseminating knowledge in the pursuit of education, learning and research at the highest international levels of excellence.

www.cambridge.org
Information on this title: www.cambridge.org/9781009311342

First published 2017
Second edition 2023

20 19 18 17 16 15 14 13 12 11 10 9 8 7 6 5

Printed in Poland by Opolgraf

A catalogue record for this publication is available from the British Library

ISBN 978-1-009-31134-2 Workbook with Digital Access

Additional resources for this publication at www.cambridge.org/9781009311342

Cambridge University Press has no responsibility for the persistence or accuracy of URLs for external or third-party internet websites referred to in this publication, and does not guarantee that any content on such websites is, or will remain, accurate or appropriate. Information regarding prices, travel timetables, and other factual information given in this work is correct at the time of first printing but Cambridge University Press does not guarantee the accuracy of such information thereafter.

....

....

Endorsement statement

Endorsement indicates that a resource has passed Cambridge International's rigorous quality-assurance process and is suitable to support the delivery of a Cambridge International syllabus. However, endorsed resources are not the only suitable materials available to support teaching and learning, and are not essential to be used to achieve the qualification. Resource lists found on the Cambridge International website will include this resource and other endorsed resources.

Any example answers to questions taken from past question papers, practice questions, accompanying marks and mark schemes included in this resource have been written by the authors and are for guidance only. They do not replicate examination papers. In examinations the way marks are awarded may be different. Any references to assessment and/or assessment preparation are the publisher's interpretation of the syllabus requirements. Examiners will not use endorsed resources as a source of material for any assessment set by Cambridge International.

While the publishers have made every attempt to ensure that advice on the qualification and its assessment is accurate, the official syllabus, specimen assessment materials and any associated assessment guidance materials produced by the awarding body are the only authoritative source of information and should always be referred to for definitive guidance. Cambridge International recommends that teachers consider using a range of teaching and learning resources based on their own professional judgement of their students' needs.

Cambridge International has not paid for the production of this resource, nor does Cambridge International receive any royalties from its sale. For more information about the endorsement process, please visit www.cambridgeinternational.org/endorsed-resources

Cambridge International copyright material in this publication is reproduced under licence and remains the intellectual property of Cambridge Assessment International Education.

Third party websites and resources referred to in this publication have not been endorsed by Cambridge Assessment International Education.

2022 CAMBRIDGE DEDICATED TEACHER AWARDS

Teachers play an important part in shaping futures. Our Dedicated Teacher Awards recognise the hard work that teachers put in every day.

Thank you to everyone who nominated this year; we have been inspired and moved by all of your stories. Well done to all of our nominees for your dedication to learning and for inspiring the next generation of thinkers, leaders and innovators.

Congratulations to our incredible winners!

WINNER

Regional Winner
Australia, New Zealand & South-East Asia

Mohd Al Khalifa Bin Mohd Affnan
Keningau Vocational College, Malaysia

Regional Winner
Europe

Dr. Mary Shiny Ponparambil Paul
Little Flower English School, Italy

Regional Winner
North & South America

Noemi Falcon
Zora Neale Hurston Elementary School, United States

Regional Winner
Central & Southern Africa

Temitope Adewuyi
Fountain Heights Secondary School, Nigeria

Regional Winner
Middle East & North Africa

Uroosa Imran
Beaconhouse School System KG-1 branch, Pakistan

Regional Winner
East & South Asia

Jeenath Akther
Chittagong Grammar School, Bangladesh

For more information about our dedicated teachers and their stories, go to
dedicatedteacher.cambridge.org

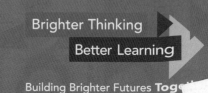

Brighter Thinking

Better Learning

Building Brighter Futures Together

› Contents

> How to use this series

We offer a comprehensive, flexible array of resources for the Cambridge IGCSE™ Combined and Co-ordinated Sciences syllabuses. We provide targeted support and practice for the specific challenges we've heard that students face: learning science with English as a second language; structured learning for all; and developing practical skills.

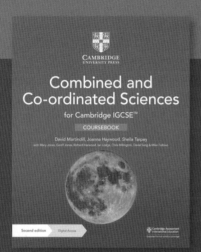

The coursebook provides coverage of the full Cambridge IGCSE™ Combined and Co-ordinated Sciences syllabuses. Each chapter explains facts and concepts, and uses relevant real-world examples of scientific principles to bring the subject to life. Together with a focus on practical work and plenty of active learning opportunities, the coursebook prepares learners for all aspects of their scientific study. Questions and practice questions in every chapter help learners to consolidate their understanding and provide practice opportunities to apply their learning.

The teacher's resource contains detailed guidance for all topics of the syllabuses, including common misconceptions identifying areas where learners might need extra support, as well as an engaging bank of lesson ideas for each syllabus topic. Differentiation is emphasised with advice for identification of different learner needs and suggestions of appropriate interventions to support and stretch learners. The teacher's resource also contains support for preparing and carrying out all the investigations in the practical workbook, including a set of sample results for when practicals aren't possible.

The teacher's resource also contains scaffolded worksheets and unit tests for each chapter. Answers for all components are accessible to teachers for free on the Cambridge Go platform.

The skills-focused workbooks have been carefully constructed to help learners develop the skills that they need as they progress through their Cambridge IGCSE™ Combined and Co-ordinated Sciences course, providing further practice of some of the topics in the coursebook, each science with its own separate workbook. A three-tier, scaffolded approach to skills development enables students to gradually progress through 'focus', 'practice' and 'challenge' exercises, ensuring that every learner is supported. The workbooks enable independent learning and are ideal for use in class or as homework.

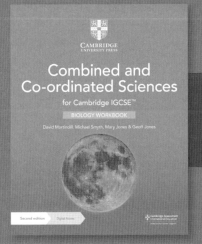

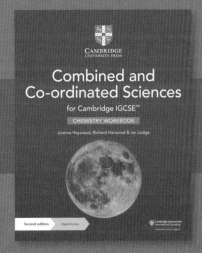

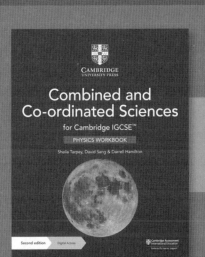

> How to use this book

Throughout this book, you will notice lots of different features that will help your learning.
These are explained below.

LEARNING INTENTIONS

These set the scene for each exercise and indicate the important concepts.

KEY WORDS

Definitions for useful vocabulary are given at the start of each section. You will also find definitions for these words in the Glossary at the back of this book.

KEY EQUATIONS

These boxes remind learners of important equations that are required to answer questions in a topic or exercise.

TIP

The information in these boxes will help you complete the exercises, and give you support in areas that you might find difficult.

Exercises

These help you to practise skills that are important for studying Cambridge IGCSE Physics.

Questions within exercises fall into one of three types:

- Focus questions will help build your basic skills.

- Practice questions provide more opportunities to test your knowledge, pushing your skills further.

- Challenge questions will stretch and challenge you even further.

SELF/PEER ASSESSMENT

At the end of some exercises, you will find opportunities to help you assess your own work, or that of your classmates, and consider how you can improve the way you learn.

> Introduction

This workbook covers two syllabuses: Cambridge IGCSE Combined Science (0653) and Cambridge IGCSE and IGCSE (9-1) Co-ordinated Sciences syllabuses (0654/0973). Before you start using this workbook, check with your teacher which syllabus you are studying and which papers you will take. You will sit either the Core paper or the Extended paper for your syllabus. If you are sitting the Extended paper, you will study the Core material and the Supplement material for your syllabus.

Once you know which paper you will be sitting, you can use the exercises in this workbook to help develop the skills you need and prepare for your examination.

The examination tests three different Assessment Objectives, or AOs for short. These are:

AO1 Knowledge with understanding

AO2 Handling information and problem solving

AO3 Experimental skills and investigations.

Just learning your work and remembering it is not enough to make sure that you achieve your best result in your exam. You also need to be able to use what you've learned in unfamiliar contexts (AO2) and to demonstrate your experimental skills (AO3).

There are lots of activities in your coursebook which will help you to develop your experimental skills by doing practical work. This workbook contains exercises to help you to develop AO2 and AO3 further. There are some questions that just involve remembering things you have been taught (AO1), but most of the questions require you to use what you've learned to work out, for example, what a set of data means, or to suggest how an experiment might be improved.

These exercises are not intended to be exactly like the questions you will get on your exam papers. This is because they are meant to help you to develop your skills, rather than testing you on them.

There's an introduction at the start of each exercise that tells you the purpose of it, and which skills you will be working with as you answer the questions.

There are sidebars in the margins of the book to show which material relates to each syllabus and paper. If there is no sidebar, it means that everyone will study this material.

Use this table to ensure that you study the right material for your syllabus and paper:

Cambridge IGCSE Combined Science (0653)		Cambridge IGCSE Co-ordinated Sciences (0654)	
Core	Supplement	Core	Supplement
You will study the material:	*You will study the material:*	*You will study the material:*	*You will study **everything**.* *You do not need to pay attention to sidebars.*
Without a sidebar	Without a sidebar With a dashed grey sidebar With a dashed black sidebar *You will <u>not</u> study material with a solid grey sidebar or a solid black sidebar.*	Without a sidebar With a solid grey sidebar With a dashed black sidebar *You will <u>not</u> study material with a solid black sidebar or a dashed grey sidebar.*	

A simplified table has also been included on the inside back flap of this workbook to open out and view alongside the exercises.

Safety

A few practical exercises have been included. These could be carried out at home using simple materials that you are likely to have available to you.

While carrying out such experiments, it is your responsibility to think about your own safety, and the safety of others. If you work sensibly and assess any risks before starting, you should come to no harm. If you are in doubt, discuss what you are going to do with your teacher before you start.

> Chapter 1
Motion

> Measuring length and volume

Exercise 1.1

IN THIS EXERCISE YOU WILL:

* recall and use the SI units used in physics.

Focus

1 **a** State the SI unit (name and symbol) for each of these quantities:

length ....

volume. ....

b State the name in words and the symbol for the following measurements:

one thousand metres ....

one-thousandth of a metre. ....

c State the number of centimetres in a metre. ....

d State the number of litres in a cubic metre. ....

Practice

2 **a** State the number of cm^2 in $1\,m^2$.

....

b State the number of m^2 in $1\,km^2$.

....

Challenge

3 A cube has sides 3.50 m long. Calculate:

a the surface area of the cube in cm²

....

....

....

....

....

b the volume of the cube in mm³.

....

....

....

....

....

> Density

Exercise 1.2

IN THIS EXERCISE YOU WILL:

- practise converting between units
- practise applying the density formula.

KEY WORD
density: the ratio of mass to volume for a substance.

KEY EQUATION

$$\text{density} = \frac{\text{mass}}{\text{volume}}$$

$$\rho = \frac{m}{V}$$

Focus

1   **a**   Table 1.1 shows data about the density of various solids and liquids.
Complete the fourth column of the table by converting each density in kg/m³
to the equivalent value in g/cm³. The first two have been done for you.

TIP

Do not assume you know the answer. Always work it out. For example, 1 m³ in mm³ is 1000 × 1000 × 1000 mm³, because there are 1000 mm in 1 m.

Material	State / type	Density / kg/m³	Density / g/cm³
water	liquid / non-metal	1000	1.000
ethanol	liquid / non-metal	800	0.800
olive oil	liquid / non-metal	920	
mercury	liquid / metal	13 500	
ice	solid / non-metal	920	
diamond	solid / non-metal	3500	
cork	solid / non-metal	250	
chalk	solid / non-metal	2700	
iron	solid / metal	7900	
tungsten	solid / metal	19 300	
aluminium	solid / metal	2700	
gold	solid / metal	19 300	

Table 1.1

b   Use the data in Table 1.1 to explain why ice floats on water.

....

....

....

c   Name *two* materials from the table (other than ice) which will float in water.

....

....

d Name *two* materials from the table which will sink in water.

....

....

Practice

2 A learner wrote: These data show that metals are denser than non-metals.
Do you agree? Explain your answer, using the data in Table 1.1.

....

....

....

....

3 Use the data in Table 1.1 to calculate:

a the mass of a block of iron which has a volume of 4.5 m³.
Show your working out. Give your answer in kg.

....

b the mass of a block of gold that measures 20 cm × 15 cm × 10 cm.
Show your working out. Give your answer in kg.

....

c the volume of an aluminium block which has a mass of 81 kg.
Show your working out. Give your answer in m³.

....

4 A metalworker finds a block of silvery metal. They weigh it and measure
its volume. Here are their results:

mass of block = 0.270 kg

volume of block = 14.0 cm³

a Calculate the density of the block.

....

....

b Suggest what metal it might be.

....

Challenge

5 Describe how you could find the density of the metal object in Figure 1.1. Include:

* the equipment you would use
* how you would use the equipment
* what you would do with the data you collect.

....

....

....

....

....

....

....

....

....

Figure 1.1: A metal object.

〉 Measuring time

Exercise 1.3

IN THIS EXERCISE YOU WILL:

* find out how good your pulse would be as a means of measuring time intervals.

Galileo used the regular pulse of his heart to measure intervals of time, until he noticed that a swinging pendulum was more reliable.

In this exercise, you need to be able to measure the pulse in your wrist. Place two fingers of one hand on the inside of the opposite wrist (see Figure 1.2). Press gently at different points until you find the pulse. Alternatively, press two fingers gently under your jawbone on either side of your neck. Safety – throughout this activity you should consider your level of fitness and not push yourself too hard.

You will also need a clock or watch that will allow you to measure intervals of time in seconds.

Figure 1.2: Two methods for taking a pulse.

Focus

1 a Start by timing 10 pulses. (Remember to start counting from zero: 0, 1, 2, 3, …, 9, 10.) Repeat this several times and record your results in the table.

b Comment on your results.

i How much do your results vary?

....

....

ii Give a possible reason for this. Is it difficult to time the pulses or does your heart rate vary?

....

....

c Use your results to calculate the average time for one pulse.

....

....

....

Practice

2 Time how long it takes for 50 pulses. Record your results in the table.

3 Calculate the average time for one pulse.

....

....

....

Challenge

4   Investigate how your pulse changes if you take some gentle exercise, for example,
by walking briskly, or by walking up and down stairs.

Write up your investigation in the lined space.

- •   Briefly describe your gentle exercise.

- •   State the measurements of pulse rate that you have made.

- •   Comment on whether you agree with Galileo that a pendulum is a better
instrument for measuring time than your pulse.

....

....

....

....

....

....

....

....

....

....

....

....

....

....

SELF ASSESSMENT

Compare your answers to those of your peers. Do you agree with their points? Are you able to justify yours?

> Understanding speed

Exercise 1.4

IN THIS EXERCISE YOU WILL:

- recall how to measure and calculate the speed of a moving object.

KEY WORDS

speed: the distance travelled by an object in unit time.

velocity: speed in a given direction.

KEY EQUATIONS

$$\text{speed} = \frac{\text{distance}}{\text{time}}$$

$$v = \frac{s}{t}$$

$$\text{average speed} = \frac{\text{total distance travelled}}{\text{total time taken}}$$

$$\text{speed} = \text{gradient of distance–time graph}$$

TIP

There are three mistakes that you can make in calculations:

- rearranging the equation incorrectly

- incorrect or missing unit conversion

- missing or incorrect units.

Practise rearranging equations until you are really confident. To check that you are doing it right, choose a calculation where you know all the quantities. For example, in this chapter, you might say 7 m/s would mean 35 metres travelled in 5 seconds. Rearrange the equation for speed to make distance the subject. Then rearrange again to make time the subject. Substitute the numbers into each rearranged equation. If you have rearranged correctly, both sides of the equation should still be equal.

Focus

1   To find the speed of an object, you can measure the time it takes to travel a known distance. Table 1.2 shows the three quantities involved.

Complete the table as follows.

- In the second column, give the SI unit for each quantity (name and symbol).
- In the third column, give one or more non-SI units for each quantity.
- In the fourth column, name suitable instruments to measure distance and time.

Quantity	SI unit (name and symbol)	Non-SI units	Measuring instrument
distance			
time			
speed			

Table 1.2

TIP

Make sure you know how to calculate the number of:

- metres in a kilometre
- seconds in an hour (or a day, or a year)
- cm^3 in a m^3.

Take care with units. Whenever you complete a calculation, remember to ask: 'What units should I have here?'.

2   There are lots of different units for speed and it is important to use an appropriate unit. Connect each measurement with the most suitable unit.

Measurement	Unit
speed of a moving car	centimetres per year
speed of movement of a tectonic plate	metres per second
speed of sound	centimetres per minute
speed at which a snail crawls	kilometres per hour

3 In the laboratory, two light gates can be used to find the speed of a moving trolley. A timer measures the time taken for the trolley to travel from one light gate to the other.

a State what other quantity must be measured to determine the trolley's speed.

....

b Write down the equation used to calculate the speed of the trolley.

....

....

c A trolley takes 0.80 s to travel between two light gates, which are separated by 2.24 m.

Calculate the average speed of the trolley.

....

....

Practice

4 The speed of moving vehicles is sometimes measured using detectors buried in the road.

The two detectors are about 1 m apart. As a vehicle passes over the first detector, an electronic timer starts. As it passes over the second detector, the timer stops.

a Explain how the vehicle's speed can then be calculated.

....

....

....

b On one stretch of road, any vehicle travelling faster than 25 m/s is breaking the speed limit.

Two detectors are placed 1.2 m apart. Calculate the speed of a car that takes 0.050 s to travel this distance. Is it breaking the speed limit?

....

....

....

c   Calculate the shortest time a car can take to travel between the detectors without breaking the speed limit.

....

....

Challenge

5   Think about the speed-detection system described in question **4**. Describe briefly how a system like this could be used to turn on a warning light whenever a speeding car goes past.

....

....

....

....

....

PEER ASSESSMENT

Compare your answer to question **5** with those of your peers. What are the best aspects of their solutions? How could they improve their solutions?

Exercise 1.5

IN THIS EXERCISE YOU WILL:

- recall and use the equation for speed
- state the difference between speed and velocity.

Focus

1   Table 1.3 shows the time taken for three cars to travel 100 m.

a   Complete the table by calculating the speed of each car. Give your answers in m/s and to one decimal place.

b Circle the fastest car in the left-hand column.

Car	Time taken / s	Speed / m/s
red car	4.2	
green car	3.8	
yellow car	4.7	

Table 1.3

2   A jet aircraft travels 1200 km in 1 h 20 min.

   a   Calculate how many metres it travels. ....

   b   Calculate the travel time in minutes and seconds. ....

   c   Calculate the travel time in seconds. ....

   d   Calculate its average speed during the flight.

   ....

3   Calculate the speed of the following moving objects. Consider the most appropriate unit to use for each object.

   a   A cheetah runs 100 m in 5 s

   ....

   ....

   ....

   b   A girl runs 800 m in 2 minutes and 40 seconds

   ....

   ....

   ....

   c   A car drives 500 km in 6 hours

   ....

   ....

   ....

Practice

4 **a** A stone falls 20 m in 2.0 s. Calculate its average speed as it falls.

....

....

b The stone falls a further 25 m in the next 1.0 s of its fall. Calculate the stone's average speed during the 3 s of its fall.

....

....

....

c Explain why we can only calculate the stone's *average* speed during its fall.

....

....

....

d State the stone's average velocity during the fall. Explain why you have stated it in this way.

....

....

Challenge

5 The microwaves used in police speed-detection devices travel at 300 000 km/s.

A pulse of microwaves emitted from the device is reflected from an object 200 m away.

Calculate how long it takes for the pulse to return to the device.

....

....

....

> **TIP**
>
> There are many applications of waves to calculate distance or speed, where the waves are reflected from an object to calculate how far away it is or how fast it is travelling.
>
> Remember that the distance travelled from source to object and back is TWICE the distance to the object.
>
> Another way to look at this is that the time for the waves to travel *from* the source to the object and back is twice the time for the waves to travel *to* the object.

Exercise 1.6

IN THIS EXERCISE YOU WILL:

- practise rearranging the equation for speed.

Focus

1 **a** A car is moving at 22 m/s. Calculate how far it will travel in 35 s.

....

....

....

b A swallow (a type of bird) can fly at 25 m/s. Calculate how long it will take to fly 1.0 km.

....

....

....

....

2 Calculate the distance travelled by each of these moving objects. Remember to check the units each time.

a A car drives at 80 km/h for 3.5 hours.

....

....

....

b An aeroplane travels at 750 km/h for 15 minutes.

....

....

....

c A cyclist rides at 4 m/s for one hour.

....

....

....

3 Calculate the time taken for each of these journeys. Remember to check the units each time.

a A car driving at 80 km/h drives 120 km.

....

....

....

b The space shuttle travelling at 2800 km/h travels 12 km.

....

....

....

c A sprinter running at 10.8 m/s completes a 100 m race.

....

....

....

Practice

4 a A high-speed train is 180 m long. It is travelling at 50 m/s. Calculate how long it will take to pass a person standing at a railway crossing.

....

....

....

....

b Calculate how long the train will take to pass completely through a station whose platforms are 220 m in length.

....

....

....

....

Challenge

5   In a 100 m race, the winner crosses the finishing line in 10.00 s.
The runner-up takes 10.20 s.

a Estimate the distance between the winner and the runner-up as the winner crosses the line. Show your method of working.

....

....

....

....

b Explain why your answer can only be an estimate.

....

....

....

Exercise 1.7

IN THIS EXERCISE YOU WILL:

- practise drawing and interpreting distance–time graphs
- perform calculations based on the graphs you have drawn.

Focus

1   Diagrams A–D in Figure 1.3 are distance–time graphs for four moving objects. Identify the graph or graphs that match each description of motion in Table 1.4. Then complete Table 1.4 by writing the correct letters in the second column.

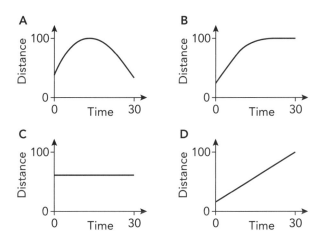

Figure 1.3: Distance–time graphs for four moving objects.

Description of motion	Graph(s)
moving at a steady speed	
stationary (not moving)	
slowing down and stopping	
changing speed	

Table 1.4

Practice

2 Table 1.5 shows the distance travelled by a runner during a 100 m race.

Distance / m	0	10.0	25.0	45.0	65.0	85.0	105.0
Time / s	0.0	2.0	4.0	6.0	8.0	10.0	12.0

Table 1.5

a Use the data in Table 1.5 to draw a distance–time graph on the graph grid below.

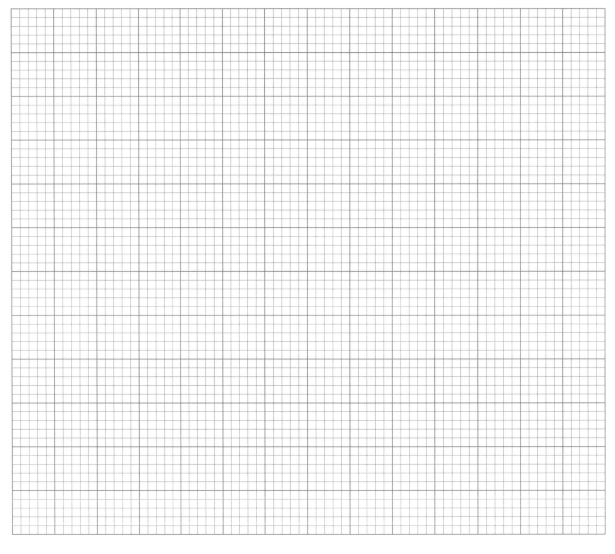

b Use your graph to answer these questions.

i Determine how far the runner travelled in the first 9.0 s.

....

ii Determine how long the runner took to run the first 50.0 m.

....

iii Determine how long the runner took to complete the 100 m.

....

c Use the gradient of your graph to determine the runner's average speed between 4.0 s and 10.0 s. Show the triangle you construct on the graph to find the gradient, where the graph forms the hypotenuse of the triangle.

....

....

....

....

3 On the graph grid below, sketch a distance–time graph for the car whose journey is described here.

- The car set off at a slow, steady speed for 20 s.

- Then it moved for 40 s at a faster speed.

- Then it stopped at traffic lights for 20 s before setting off again at a slow, steady speed.

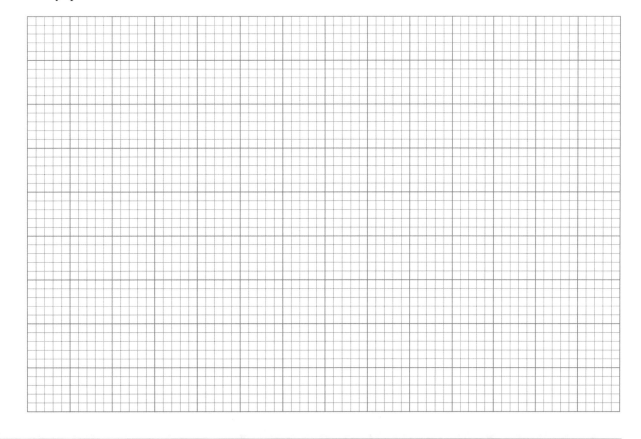

Challenge

4 The graph in Figure 1.4 represents the motion of a bus for part of a journey.

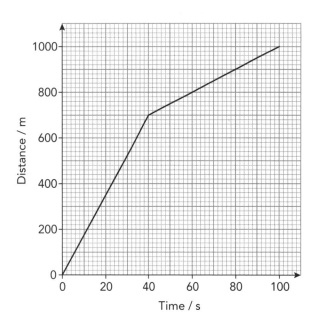

Figure 1.4: Distance–time graph for a bus.

a On the graph in Figure 1.4, mark the section of the journey where the bus was moving more quickly.

b Using Figure 1.4, calculate:

i the speed of the bus when it was moving more quickly

....

....

ii the average speed of the bus.

....

....

› Understanding acceleration
Exercise 1.8

IN THIS EXERCISE YOU WILL:

- check that you understand acceleration
- recall the equation for acceleration
- practise using the equation for acceleration.

KEY EQUATIONS

$$acceleration = \frac{change\ in\ velocity}{time}$$

$$a = \frac{\Delta v}{\Delta t}$$

acceleration = gradient of speed–time graph

distance = area under speed–time graph

KEY WORDS

acceleration: the rate of change of an object's velocity.

deceleration: negative acceleration (the rate of decrease of velocity).

TIP

In an equation, the Greek letter delta Δ represents 'change'. In the equation to determine acceleration, acceleration (a) = change in velocity (Δv) over the time taken, or change in time (Δt).

Focus

1   In an advertisement, a car is described like this:

'It can accelerate from 0 km/h to 80 km/h in 10 s.'

Calculate the average increase in the speed of the car per second.

....

Practice

2   A cyclist is travelling at 4.0 m/s. She speeds up to 16 m/s in a time of 5.6 s. Calculate her acceleration.

....

....

....

3   A stone falls with an acceleration of 9.8 m/s^2. Calculate its speed after falling for 3.5 s.

....

....

4   On the Moon, gravity is weaker than on Earth. A stone falls on the Moon with an acceleration of 1.6 m/s^2. Calculate how long it will take to reach a speed of 10 m/s.

....

....

Challenge

5   On Earth, the acceleration of free fall is 9.8 m/s^2. On Pluto, the acceleration due to gravity is 0.62 m/s^2. A stone is thrown upwards on Earth, leaving the ground at 10 m/s. This is then repeated on Pluto. Calculate how much longer the stone takes to land on Pluto. Ignore air resistance in your calculations.

....

....

Exercise 1.9

IN THIS EXERCISE YOU WILL:

- draw and interpret some speed–time graphs

- calculate the acceleration of an object from the gradient (slope) of the graph

- calculate the distance travelled from the area under the graph.

Focus

1   Diagrams A–D in Figure 1.5 show speed–time graphs for four moving objects. Identify the graph or graphs that match each description of motion in Table 1.6. Then complete Table 1.6 by writing the correct letters in the second column.

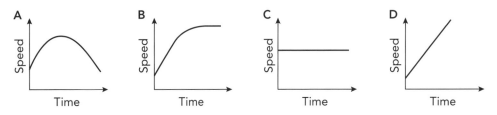

Figure 1.5: Speed–time graphs for four moving objects.

Description of motion	Graph(s)
moving at a steady speed	
speeding up, then slowing down	
moving with constant acceleration	
accelerating to a steady speed	

Table 1.6

2 The graph in Figure 1.6 represents the motion of a car that accelerates from rest and then travels at a steady speed.

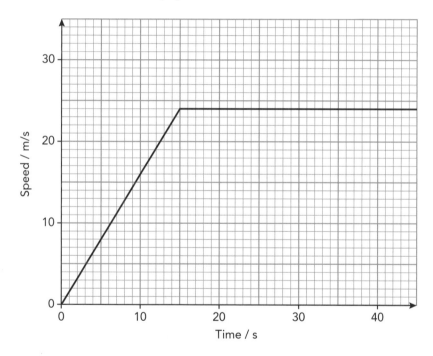

Figure 1.6: Speed–time graph for a car.

Use Figure 1.6 to determine the acceleration of the car in the first part of its journey.

....

Practice

3 **a** On Figure 1.6, shade the area that represents the distance travelled by the car while accelerating. Label this area A.

b Shade the area that represents the distance travelled by the car at a steady speed. Label this area B.

c Remember: area of a triangle $= \dfrac{1}{2} \times$ base $\times$ height
Calculate:

i the distance travelled by the car while accelerating

....

....

ii the distance travelled by the car at a steady speed

....

....

iii the total distance travelled by the car.

....

....

Challenge

4 On the graph grid below, sketch a speed–time graph for the car journey described here.

- The car travels at a slow, steady speed for 20 s.

- Then, during a time of 10 s, it accelerates to a faster speed.

- It travels at this steady speed for 20 s.

- Then it rapidly decelerates and comes to a stop after 10 s.

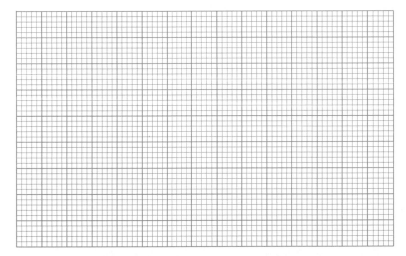

Exercise 1.10

Focus

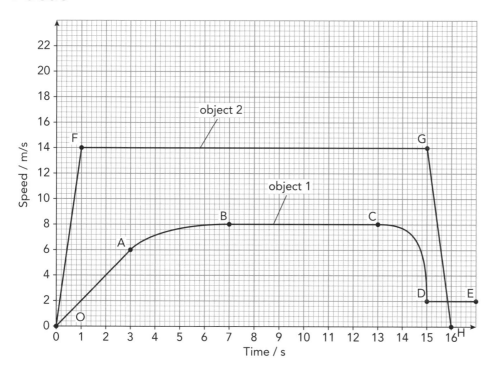

Figure 1.7: The motion of two objects. The motion of object 1 is shown through points A–E. The motion of object 2 is shown through points F–H. Point O is (0,0).

1   Describe the motion of object 1 in Figure 1.7:

   a   between O and A

   ....

   b   between A and B

   ....

   c   between B and C

   ....

   d   between C and D

....

   e   between D and E.

....

Practice

2   Calculate the acceleration of object 1 in Figure 1.7:

   a   between O and A

....

   b   between A and B

....

   c   between B and C

....

   d   between C and D

....

   e   between D and E

....

   f   at exactly 14 seconds.

....

Challenge

3   The two objects in Figure 1.7 are cars in a race.

   a   Explain the shape of section AB.

....

....

....

....

b The cars are racing each other. Explain the differences between object 1's motion between O and C and object 2's motion between O and G.

....

....

....

....

⟩ Mass, weight and gravity
Exercise 1.11

KEY EQUATIONS

gravitational field strength = force per unit mass

$$g = \frac{W}{m}$$

KEY WORDS

mass: a measure of the quantity of matter in an object at rest relative to the observer.

weight: the downward force of gravity that acts on an object because of its mass.

Focus

1 State the accepted value of the gravitational field strength on Earth.

....

....

2 a State the equation that connects mass, weight and gravitational field strength.

....

b State the name of the instrument we use in a laboratory to measure weight.

....

Practice

3 The gravitational field strength on Earth is 9.8 N/kg.

Use this to calculate the weight of the following objects on Earth:

a a 50 kg girl

....

....

....

b a 1500 kg car

....

....

....

c a 440 g can of beans

....

....

....

d a spider with a mass of 1 mg.

....

....

....

4 The gravitational field strength on Mars is approximately 4 N/kg. On Jupiter, the gravitational field strength is approximately 23 N/kg. A boy weighs 700 N on Earth. Calculate:

a the boy's mass

....

....

....

b the boy's weight on Mars

....

....

....

c the boy's weight on Jupiter.

....

....

....

5 The International Space Station (ISS) orbits at the outer edge of the Earth's atmosphere. It is often said that astronauts in the ISS are weightless. State whether you think this is true. Explain your answer.

....

....

....

....

....

PEER ASSESSMENT

Compare your answers to those of your peers. Have they covered all the relevant points? Have you? How could they improve their answers?

Challenge

6 Figure 1.8 shows a man indoor skydiving. In the picture, he is floating, stationary. Imagine the same man floating in deep space. Compare the forces required to move him horizontally in a building on Earth and in deep space. Ignore any difference due to the space suit he would wear in space. Explain your answer.

....

....

....

....

Figure 1.8: Indoor skydiving.

7   Imagine a creature that lived on Jupiter came to Earth and competed in the Olympic high jump. Consider how they are likely to perform against human competitors and explain your answer. You may want to find out the value of the gravitational field strength on Jupiter.

....

....

....

....

....

....

> Forces

Exercise 1.12

IN THIS EXERCISE YOU WILL:

- practise identifying forces, drawing arrows to represent their sizes and their directions.

KEY WORDS

force: the action of one body on a second body that causes its velocity to change.

resultant force: the single force that has the same effect on a body as two or more forces.

Focus

1   Fill in the blanks.

A force can change the _____, _____ and

_____ of an object.

Practice

2   Figure 1.9 shows some bodies (objects). Add at least one force arrow to each body, showing a force acting on it. Two force arrows are already shown.

Each force arrow should be labelled to indicate the following:

- the type of force (contact, drag/air resistance, weight/gravitational, push/pull, friction, magnetic)
- the body causing the force
- the body acted on by the force.

For example, for part **a**: the gravitational force of the Earth on the apple.

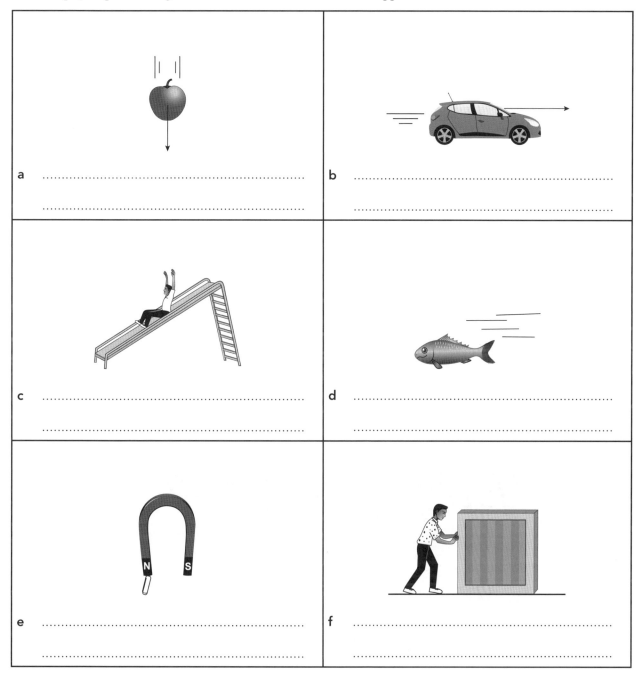

a ....

....

b ....

....

c ....

....

d ....

....

e ....

....

f ....

....

Figure 1.9: Six situations where forces are acting.

Challenge

3   Why does Figure 1.10 seem to show an impossible situation?

....

....

....

4   Using your knowledge of forces, draw arrows on Figure 1.10 to show where the
     forces are acting.

Figure 1.10: Why does this seem impossible?

Exercise 1.13

IN THIS EXERCISE YOU WILL:

- practise applying your knowledge to predict the effect of forces
  on objects.

Focus

1   Each diagram in Figure 1.11 shows a body (object) with a single force acting on it.
     State what effect the force will have in each case.

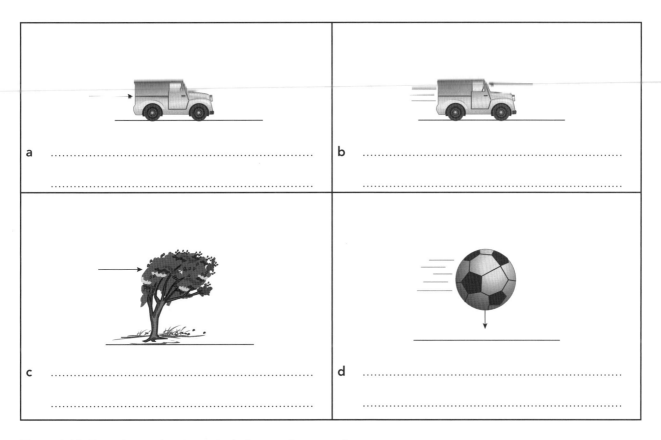

Figure 1.11: Four objects showing a single force acting on each one.

Practice

2 A boy slides down a sloping ramp.

   a In the space below, draw a diagram of the boy on the ramp in the space below. Add a labelled arrow to show the force of friction that acts on him.

b Describe the effect the force will have on the boy's movement.

....

....

c State the other effect of friction between two surfaces.

....

....

Challenge

3 A girl drops her phone from a low height. It lands on the ground but it does not break. If she drops it from a first-floor window on to the ground, it does break. Since the weight of the phone has not changed, explain why this is true.

....

....

Exercise 1.14

IN THIS EXERCISE YOU WILL:

- practise working out the resultant force due to several forces acting on an object.

Focus

1 The left-hand column of Table 1.7 shows two objects acted on by different forces. In the right-hand column, draw a force arrow to show the resultant force acting on each object. Label the arrow with the size of the resultant force.

Forces on object	Resultant force
80 N → ☐ ← 45 N	☐
60 N ← ☐ ← 40 N 50 N →	☐

Table 1.7

Practice

2 Describe an effect that a resultant force will have on the motion of an object, for example, a car.

....

3 Describe the motion of the object if the resultant force falls to zero.

....

4 A car's engine produces a force of 2000 N. The force of air resistance on the car is 800 N.

    a In the space below, sketch the car and draw force arrows to show these forces acting on the car.

    b What is the resultant force on the car?

....

    c Describe how the car will move.

....

    d The driver of the car takes their foot off the accelerator, so the engine no longer exerts a force. Describe and explain what will happen to the car.

....

....

....

Challenge

5 In the space below, draw a diagram showing a body (object) with four forces acting on it. Their resultant must be 4 N acting vertically downwards.

> Force, mass and acceleration

Exercise 1.15

IN THIS EXERCISE YOU WILL:

- practise using the relationship that connects resultant force, mass and acceleration.

KEY EQUATION

force = mass × acceleration

$F = ma$

Focus

1 a Complete Table 1.8 to show the names of these quantities and their SI units.

Quantity	Symbol	SI unit
	F	
	m	
	a	

Table 1.8

b State the equation that connects these three quantities, with F as the subject.

....

c Rearrange the equation to make m the subject.

$m =$ ....

d Rearrange the equation to make a the subject.

$a =$ ....

Practice

2 Calculate the resultant force needed to give a mass of 20 kg an acceleration of 0.72 m/s².

....

....

....

3 A resultant force of 1575 N acts on a car of mass 450 kg. Calculate the acceleration of the car.

....

....

....

4 One way to find the mass of an object is to apply a force to it and measure its acceleration. An astronaut pushes on a spacecraft with a force of 200 N. The spacecraft accelerates at 0.12 m/s². Calculate the mass of the spacecraft.

....

....

....

Challenge

5 a In the space below, draw a falling stone with the following forces acting on it:

- its weight, 8.0 N
- air resistance, 2.4 N.

b The mass of the stone is 0.80 kg. Calculate its acceleration.

....

....

> Stretching springs

Exercise 1.16

IN THIS EXERCISE YOU WILL:

- describe an experiment to investigate the relationship between the load on a spring and the extension of that spring
- practise plotting a graph and drawing conclusions from it.

KEY EQUATION

$$\text{spring constant} = \frac{\text{force}}{\text{unit extension}}$$

$$k = \frac{F}{x}$$

KEY WORDS

extension: the increase in length of an object (for example, a spring) when a load (for example, a weight) is attached to it.

limit of proportionality: up to this limit, the extension on a spring is proportional to load.

Focus

1 Describe how you would carry out an experiment to investigate the relationship between the load on a spring and the extension of that spring. In the space below, draw a diagram of your experimental arrangement.

....

....

....

....

....

KEY WORDS

load: the force (usually weight) that stretches an object (a spring).

spring constant: the constant of proportionality; the measure of the stiffness of a spring.

Practice

2 a A learner carried out an experiment to stretch a spring. Table 1.9 shows their results. Complete the third column of the table.

Load / N	Length / cm	Extension / mm
0	25.0	
1.0	25.4	
2.0	25.8	
3.0	26.2	
4.0	26.6	
5.0	27.0	
6.0	27.4	
7.0	27.8	
8.0	28.5	
9.0	29.2	
10.0	29.9	

Table 1.9

> **TIP**
>
> Remember that the extension is the **total** increase in length from the unstretched value.

b Use the data in Table 1.9 to estimate the force needed to produce an extension of 1.0 cm.

....

c   On the graph grid, draw an extension–load graph for the spring.

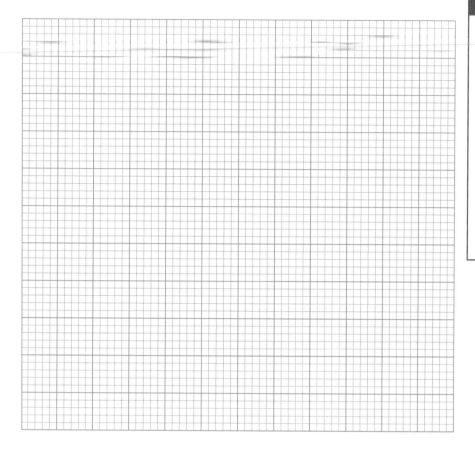

TIP

Plotting graphs is a skill that requires practice. Plan before you begin. Choose a scale that will allow your points to fill at least half the graph paper in each direction. Make sure your scale will make it easy to read off values between the points. Plot in pencil, so you can correct mistakes.

Challenge

3   a   Calculate the gradient of the straight part of your graph from question **2**.
Comment on what it means.

....

....

....

....

b   From your graph, estimate the load at the limit of proportionality.

....

TIP

When you calculate a gradient, always ask: 'What should the units of this value be?' This will help you to use appropriate units and to understand what the gradient actually means.

❯ Turning forces

Exercise 1.17

IN THIS EXERCISE YOU WILL:
• check your understanding of simple turning effects and of equilibrium.

KEY EQUATION
moment of a force = force × perpendicular distance from pivot to force

KEY WORDS

centre of gravity: the point at which the mass of an object can be considered to be concentrated.

equilibrium: when no net force and no net moment act on a body.

moment of a force: the turning effect of a force about a point.

Focus

1 Figure 1.12 shows a playground see-saw. Explain how a see-saw like this can balance.

....

....

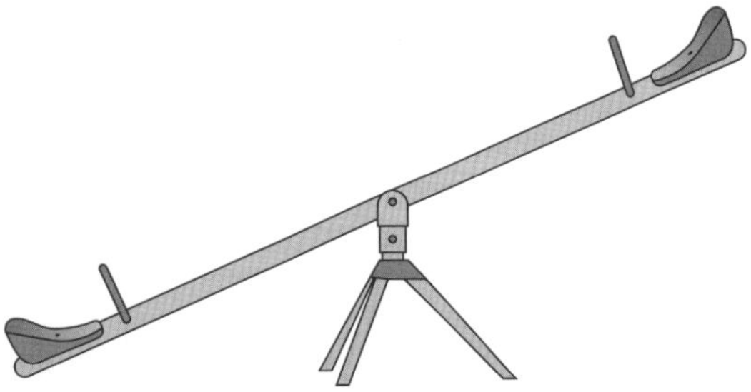

Figure 1.12: A playground see-saw.

2 A body (object) is in equilibrium.

  a State the resultant force on the body.

....

  b State the resultant turning effect on the body.

....

Practice

3 Figure 1.13 shows a wheelbarrow with a heavy load of soil.

a Add an arrow to the diagram to show how you could lift the left hand end of the barrow with the smallest force possible. Remember to indicate clearly the direction of the force.

Figure 1.13: A wheelbarrow.

b How do you know that the wheelbarrow is in equilibrium?

....

Challenge

4 Figure 1.14 shows a beam balanced on a pivot.

a Add arrows to show the following forces:

- A 100 N force pressing downwards on the beam that will have the greatest possible clockwise turning effect. Label this force A.

- A 200 N force pressing downwards on the beam that will have an anticlockwise turning effect equal in size to the turning effect of force A. Label this force B.

Figure 1.14: A uniform beam, balanced on a pivot at the centre of the beam.

b As well as forces A and B, what other forces are acting to keep the beam in equilibrium?

....

....

c   Why can we ignore these forces when calculating moments about the pivot?

....

Exercise 1.18

IN THIS EXERCISE YOU WILL:

• check your understanding of how to calculate moments.

Focus

1   Fill in the blanks in the sentence below.

The _____ of a force is the turning effect of the force. It is calculated by

multiplying the size of the force by the _____ distance of the _____

from the pivot.

Practice

2   In Figure 1.15, all the forces are of equal size.

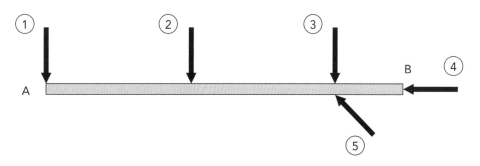

Figure 1.15: Five forces of equal size, acting at different points along a uniform beam.

a   State the force with the greatest moment about point A. ....

b   State the force that has no moment about point B. ....

> **TIP**
>
> Remember: We add all the clockwise moments together and add all the anticlockwise moments together. This is the key thing – *not* whether the forces are on the left or the right of the pivot. For example, a force on the left of the pivot will have a clockwise moment if it acts upwards, but an anticlockwise moment if it acts downwards.

Challenge

3   Figure 1.16 shows three forces acting on a uniform beam. Calculate the moment about the pivot of each force. Write your answers in Table 1.10.

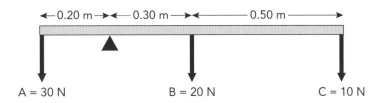

Figure 1.16: A uniform beam pivoted off-centre.

Force	Moment / N m	Clockwise or anticlockwise?
A		
B		
C		

Table 1.10

Exercise 1.19

IN THIS EXERCISE YOU WILL:

•   apply the principle of moments.

Focus

1   State the *two* conditions required for an object to be in equilibrium.

....

....

Practice

2   Two people are on a see-saw.

Person A weighs 300 N and is 1.5 m from the pivot.

Person B weighs 400 N and is 1.2 m from the pivot.

a   In the space below, draw a diagram of this situation.

b   Calculate the moment of each person.

....

....

c   State whether the see-saw is in equilibrium.

....

d   Describe what will happen to the see-saw.

....

Challenge

3 Figure 1.17 shows three beams with forces acting on them. For each situation, calculate the missing force or distance so that the beam is in equilibrium

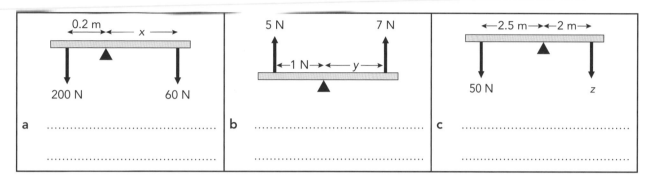

a ....

....

b ....

....

c ....

....

Figure 1.17: Three situations, showing beams balanced with different combinations of moments.

Exercise 1.20

IN THIS EXERCISE YOU WILL:

• check your understanding of stability and the factors that affect it.

Focus

1 State and explain the condition that means an object will topple (fall over).

....

....

....

....

Practice

2 Figure 1.18 shows an object that is fairly stable. Its centre of gravity is marked with a dot.

Figure 1.18: A stone on a flat surface.

   a   On the left of this object, draw an object that is more stable.
        Mark its approximate centre of gravity.

   b   On the right of this object, draw an object that is less stable.
        Mark its approximate centre of gravity.

3   Figure 1.19 shows two objects that are not very stable. The centre of gravity of
      each object is marked with a dot.

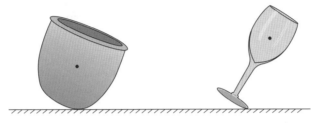

Figure 1.19: A plant pot and a water glass, both tilted to one side.

State the two vertical forces that act on each object.

Upward force: ....

Downward force: ....

4   **a**   Draw arrows on each object in Figure 1.19 to show the two forces acting on it.

     b   Decide whether each object in Figure 1.19 will fall over.
         Explain your answer.

       ....

       ....

       ....

       ....

       ....

       ....

       ....

       ....

       ....

       ....

TIP

Whether or not an object topples (falls over) depends on the moment of the weight. If this moment pulls the object further over, it will topple; if the moment causes the object to fall back, it will not topple.

Think about the line along which the object's weight acts. If this line falls outside the base of the object as it starts to fall over, the object will topple. If it falls inside the base of the object, then it tends to pull the object back onto its base so it does not topple.

Challenge

5   Use your knowledge and understanding from this chapter to design a base for a
wind turbine. Consider how you will make it stable and explain why your ideas
will achieve this. You could sketch your idea in the space provided.

PEER ASSESSMENT

Compare your answer to those of your peers. Is there anything they could add
to improve their answers? Is there anything you could have added?

〉 Pressure

Exercise 1.21

IN THIS EXERCISE YOU WILL:

- practise carrying out pressure calculations
- apply your knowledge of the pressure equation to real situations.

KEY WORD

pressure: the force
acting per unit area at
right angles to
a surface.

KEY EQUATION

$$\text{pressure} = \frac{\text{force}}{\text{area}}$$

$$p = \frac{F}{A}$$

Focus

1 The equation $p = \dfrac{F}{A}$ is used to calculate pressure.

a Complete Table 1.11 to show the name and SI unit (name and symbol) of each quantity.

Quantity	Symbol	SI unit
	F	
	p	
	A	

Table 1.11

b Rearrange the equation to make F the subject.

$F = $ ....

c Rearrange the equation to make A the subject.

$A = $ ....

2 It is dangerous to stand on the icy surface of a frozen pond or lake.

a Explain why it is more dangerous to stand on one foot than on both feet.

....

....

....

b Describe how a wild animal could move across the ice in a way that would minimise the danger of falling through.

....

....

3 Explain the following:

a A mountain bike which can be ridden over muddy fields has larger, wider tyres than a road bike.

....

....

b Snowshoes like those shown in Figure 1.20 can be fitted to shoes or boots and make it much easier to walk in snow.

....

....

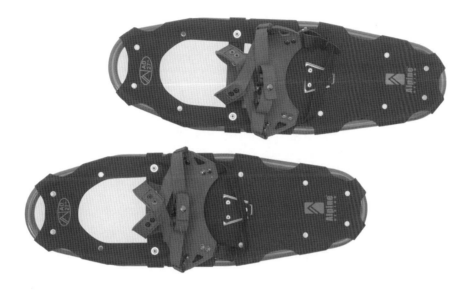

Figure 1.20: Snowshoes.

4 An elephant has a mass of 6000 kg. Each of its feet has an area of approximately 2000 cm². Calculate the pressure (in pascals) exerted on the floor by the elephant:

a if it stands on one foot

....

....

b if it stands on two feet

....

....

c if it stands on all four feet.

....

....

Practice

5 Calculate the pressure when a force of 200 N presses on an area of 0.40 m².

....

....

6 The pressure inside a car tyre is 250 kPa (250 000 Pa). Calculate the total force exerted on the inner surface of the tyre if its surface area is 0.64 m².

....

....

....

Challenge

7 A rectangular block has sides measuring 8 cm, 5 cm and 4 cm. Its mass is 1.2 kg.

    a Calculate the weight of the block. (The gravitational field strength is 9.8 N/kg.)

....

....

....

    b Calculate the volume of the block. Give your answer in cm³.

....

....

....

    c Calculate the density of the material from which the block is made. Give your answer in g/cm³.

....

....

....

d On which side should the block rest to give the minimum pressure?

....

....

....

e Calculate the pressure (in Pa) when the block is resting on the side stated in part **d**.

....

....

....

f On which side should the block rest to give the maximum pressure?

....

....

....

g Calculate the pressure when the block is resting on the side stated in part **f**.

....

....

....

> Chapter 2

Energy, work and power

> Energy stores, transfers and conservation

Exercise 2.1

IN THIS EXERCISE YOU WILL:

- check that you know what energy stores and transfers are
- practise identifying energy stores and transfers in everyday situations
- apply the principle of conservation of energy
- check that you understand the concept of efficiency.

KEY EQUATIONS

$$\text{efficiency of a device} = \frac{\text{useful energy output}}{\text{total energy input}} \times 100\%$$

$$\text{efficiency of a device} = \frac{\text{useful power output}}{\text{total power input}} \times 100\%$$

TIP

Efficiency is the proportion (*not* the amount) of total input that is transferred usefully.

You will see this expressed in terms of energy, work and power, but work and energy are the same thing and power is the rate of doing work. To decide what is useful, ask yourself: 'What is the purpose of this device?' For example, a light bulb exists to produce light so the thermal energy it produces is not generally considered useful.

KEY WORDS

chemical potential energy: energy stored in chemical substances and which can be released in a chemical reaction.

efficiency: the fraction of energy that is transferred to a useful form.

elastic (strain) energy: energy stored in the changed shape of an object.

energy: quantity that must be changed or transferred to make something happen.

gravitational potential energy: energy stored in an object that is raised up against the force of gravity.

internal energy: the energy of an object; the total kinetic and potential energies of its particles.

Focus

1 Complete Table 2.1 to show the energy stored in each situation. The first example has been done for you.

Description	Store of energy
energy in a stretched spring/elastic	elastic potential
energy in the nucleus of a uranium atom	
energy in diesel fuel	
energy of a ball held above your head	
energy of a hot cup of coffee	

Table 2.1

2 Figure 2.1 shows a rocket being launched into space, and the energy transfers that are involved.

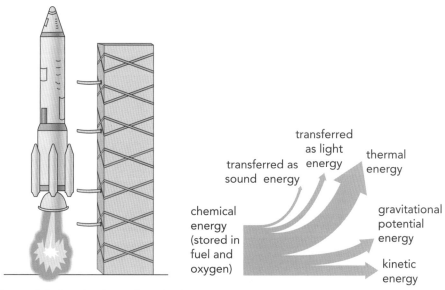

Figure 2.1: A rocket being launched.

KEY WORDS

kinetic energy: energy stored in a moving object.

nuclear potential energy: energy stored in the nucleus of an atom.

principle of conservation of energy: the total energy of interacting objects is constant provided no net external force acts.

thermal energy: energy transferred from a hotter place to a colder place because of the temperature difference between them.

In Table 2.2, explain how you know that each of these energy changes is happening. The first one has been done for you.

Energy transfer: chemical energy to …	How we can tell
sound	The rocket launch is very noisy.
light	
thermal energy	
gravitational potential energy	
kinetic energy	

Table 2.2

Practice

3 A child eats their breakfast, then takes the bus to school. At school, they climb the stairs to their classroom on the top floor.

   a Identify *two* stores of chemical energy.

   ....

   b Identify the energy store the child increases as they climb the stairs.

   ....

   c Describe the energy transfers which occur as the bus is travelling.

   ....

   ....

4 A washing machine has a motor that turns the drum. In a particular washing machine, the motor is supplied with 1500 J of energy each second. Of this, 1200 J of energy is used to turn the drum. The rest is wasted as thermal energy. Calculate the amount of energy wasted by the motor as heat each second.

   ....

Challenge

5   Calculate the efficiency of the motor in question **4**.

....

....

6   A learner argues that a car running on petrol or diesel is more efficient in winter than in summer. Explain why the learner might say this.

....

....

....

7   Each second, a gas-fired power station is supplied with 1000 MJ of energy and produces 450 MJ of electrical energy.

Each second, a coal-fired power station is supplied with 600 MJ of energy and produces 150 MJ of electrical energy.

a   Which power station is more efficient? ....

b   Calculate the efficiency of each power station.

....

....

SELF ASSESSMENT

Compare your working and answer to those of your peers. Have they missed anything? Have you?

> Energy calculations

Exercise 2.2

IN THIS EXERCISE YOU WILL:

- recall and use the equations to calculate kinetic energy and change in gravitational potential energy

- apply these equations with the principle of conservation of energy to more complex problems (see question **5**).

KEY EQUATIONS

$\text{kinetic energy} = \dfrac{1}{2} \times \text{mass} \times \text{speed}^2$

$E_k = \dfrac{1}{2}mv^2$

$\text{change in gravitational potential energy} = \text{weight} \times \text{change in height}$

$\Delta E_p = mg\Delta h$

Focus

1 Rearrange the equations for kinetic energy and change in gravitational potential energy, to make mass the subject for each one.

 a kinetic energy: $m = $ ....

 b change in gravitational potential energy: $m = $ ....

Practice

2 Calculate the kinetic energy of a car of mass 600 kg travelling at 25 m/s.

 ....

3 A walker carrying a 20 kg backpack climbs to the top of a mountain that is 2500 m high. Calculate the gain in gravitational potential energy of the pack. (Gravitational field strength, $g = 9.8$ N/kg).

 ....

TIP

Remember that, when you are calculating the change in kinetic energy, when an object goes from v_1 m/s to v_2 m/s, it is

$\dfrac{1}{2}mv_2^2 - \dfrac{1}{2}mv_1^2,$

not

$\dfrac{1}{2}m(v_2 - v_1)^2.$

Challenge

4   The car in question **2** slows down to a speed of 12 m/s. By how much has its kinetic energy decreased?

....

5   A girl throws a ball upwards, as shown in Figure 2.2. The ball has a mass of 0.20 kg and it leaves her hand with a speed of 8.0 m/s. Determine how high it will rise.

Figure 2.2: A girl throwing a ball into the air.

....

....

....

> **TIP**
>
> **Step 1:** Calculate the E_k of the ball as it leaves the girl's hand.
>
> **Step 2:** When the ball reaches its highest point, it no longer has any E_k and its energy has been transferred to E_p.
>
> We can write:
>
> E_p at highest point = E_k at lowest point
>
> $mgh = E_k$
>
> Rearranging gives:
>
> $h = \dfrac{E_k}{mg}$

6   In a game, a toy car, which is initially stationary, slides down a slope. The top of the slope is 2.0 m higher than the foot of the slope. Determine how fast the car will be moving when it reaches the foot. (Assume that all of its E_p is transferred to E_k).

....

....

....

> Energy resources

Exercise 2.3

IN THIS EXERCISE YOU WILL:

- recall which resources are renewable and non-renewable
- discuss the advantages and disadvantages of different types of energy resources.

Focus

1 Complete Table 2.3 as follows:

- In the second column, write the name of the type of energy resource.
- In the third column, indicate whether the resource is renewable or non-renewable.

The first example has been done for you.

Description	Energy resource	Renewable or non-renewable?
wood	biofuel	renewable
natural gas		
coal		
splitting of uranium nuclei		
hydrogen nuclei combine to release energy		
sunlight captured to make electricity or heat water		
hot rocks underground used to heat water		
moving air turns a turbine		
water running downhill turns a turbine		

Table 2.3

KEY WORDS

biomass fuel: a material, recently living, used as a fuel.

fossil fuel: a material formed from long-dead material, used as a fuel.

geothermal: the energy stored in hot rocks underground.

non-renewable: energy resource which, once used, is gone forever.

nuclear fission: the process by which energy is released by the splitting of a large heavy nucleus into two or more lighter nuclei.

nuclear fusion: the process by which energy is released by the joining together of two small light nuclei to form a new, heavier nucleus.

renewable: energy resource which, when used, will be replenished naturally.

TIP

Renewable is about being able to replace something at least as fast as we use it. It is *not* about being able to re-use it.

Practice

2   List *two* advantages and two disadvantages of using solar power.

....

....

....

....

Challenge

3   Compare the energy resources by completing Table 2.4. You will need to conduct research to find much of the missing information.

Resource	Renewable?	Cost per MWh of electricity	Environmental impact	Reliability
nuclear fission				
solar				
geothermal				
hydroelectric				
wind				
wave				
tidal				

Table 2.4

Exercise 2.4

IN THIS EXERCISE YOU WILL:

- consider wind power in some detail.

Focus

1   Figure 2.3 shows how much electricity was generated worldwide from the
    wind from 1996 to 2018. (The units of energy are GWh or gigawatt-hours.
    One gigawatt is 10^9 watts.) Table 2.5 shows the ten countries that contributed most
    to this total in 2018.

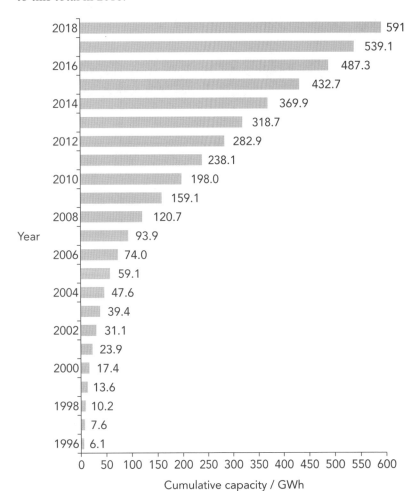

Figure 2.3: Graph of global wind power capacity.

Country	Global wind power 2018/%
China	44.3
United States	14.7
Germany	6.1
India	4.2
United Kingdom	4

Country	Global wind power 2018/%
Brazil	3.7
France	3
Mexico	1.8
Sweden	1.4
Canada	1.1

Table 2.5 *Source: Global Wind Energy Council*

Study Figure 2.3 and Table 2.5, then read each of the statements below.
Decide whether each statement is TRUE or FALSE. If a statement is FALSE,
cross out the incorrect word(s) and write the correct word(s) in the space below.
Here is an example to help you:

The amount of electricity generated from the wind reached 50 GWh in ~~2001~~. 2005		~~TRUE~~/FALSE
i	The amount of electricity generated from the wind has increased every year since 1996.	TRUE/FALSE
ii	The amount of electricity generated from the wind exceeded 100 GWh in 2006.	TRUE/FALSE
iii	The amount of electricity generated from the wind doubled between 2002 and 2005.	TRUE/FALSE
iv	The top three countries generate more than 50% of the world's wind energy.	TRUE/FALSE
v	The UK makes less use of wind energy than France.	TRUE/FALSE

Practice

2   Think about the area where you live. Suggest a good place to put a wind turbine
to generate as much electricity as possible. Give reasons for your suggestion.

....

....

....

....

Challenge

3   State objections that might be raised to using wind power as a major source of
our electricity.

....

....

....

....

....

....

Exercise 2.5

IN THIS EXERCISE YOU WILL:

- describe the energy we get directly and indirectly from the Sun in some detail
- discuss the difference between nuclear fission and nuclear fusion and how we might use nuclear fusion on Earth to generate electricity in the future.

TIP
Take care not to confuse the spelling of 'fission' and 'fusion'. Fusion spelled 'fussion' is neither one nor the other!

Focus

1 What do we use to transfer the energy from the Sun into electricity?

    ....

2 In Table 2.6, the first column lists some energy resources. In the second column, add a tick (✓) if the energy of the resource comes originally from the Sun. Add a cross (✗) if it does not. The first one has been done for you.

Energy resource	Originally from the Sun?
wood	✓
fossil fuels	
nuclear power	
tidal power	
wind power	
hydroelectric power	
wave power	
geothermal	
sunlight	

Table 2.6

Practice

3 Explain why, when we burn coal, the energy released originally came from the Sun.

....

....

....

....

....

4 The processes of fission and fusion release energy when changes happen in the nuclei of atoms. Table 2.7 lists some features of these processes. Some relate to fission and some to fusion.

Write 'fission' or 'fusion' or 'both' in the second column of the table as appropriate.

Feature	Fission, fusion or both?
large nuclei split into two	
two small nuclei join together	
energy is released	
used in a uranium-fuelled power station	
the energy source of the Sun	
helium can be a product	

Table 2.7

Challenge

5 Describe the main issues with using solar energy to generate the Earth's electricity.

....

....

....

....

....

....

....

› Doing work

Exercise 2.6

IN THIS EXERCISE YOU WILL:

* check your understanding of work

* practise explaining the energy transfers involved when work is done in some everyday situations.

KEY EQUATIONS

mechanical work done = force × distance moved by the force

$$W = F \times d = \Delta E$$

Focus

1 State the relationship between work and energy.

....

KEY WORDS

doing work: transferring energy.

energy: the capacity to do work.

joule (J): the SI unit of work or energy.

work done: the amount of energy transferred.

TIP

You will come across work, energy and power in different areas of the course, but they are the same every time you see them. Work and energy are just two words for the same thing. Power is the rate of doing work, which is the rate of energy transfer.

Practice

2 Complete these sentences:

An apple falls from a tree. The force acting on the apple to make it fall is

_____ .

As the apple falls, its speed _____ . This shows that its _____

energy store is increasing.

If this increase is by 2.0 joules (J), the work done on it is _____ J.

3 The girl in Figure 2.4 is raising a heavy load.

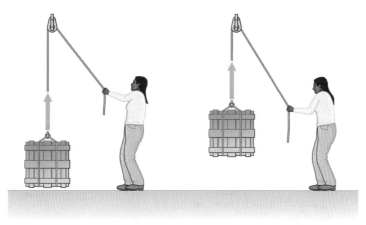

Figure 2.4: A girl lifting a heavy load using a pulley.

a Explain how you can tell that the load's energy is increasing.

....

....

b Explain where this energy comes from.

....

....

c Explain how the energy is transferred to the load.

....

....

4   In Figure 2.5, the 20 N force does more work than the 10 N force.
    How can you tell? State *two* ways.

Figure 2.5: The forces acting on a block.

....

....

....

....

Challenge

5   Using the concept of work, explain why it is more difficult to walk on an icy
    surface than on a clean, dry, unfrozen surface.

....

....

....

....

....

Exercise 2.7

Focus

1   The learner in Figure 2.6 is pulling a load up a slope.

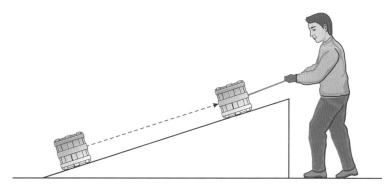

Figure 2.6: A learner pulling a load up a slope.

a   What instrument could be used to measure the force F that pulls the load?

....

b   On Figure 2.6, mark the distance x that must be measured in order to calculate the work done by the force.

c   Write the equation used to calculate the work done by the force.

....

d   The learner changes the angle of the slope four times. In the space below, draw a suitable table that could be used to record the measurements and to calculate the work done by the force.

Practice

2 A boy pushes a heavy box along the ground. His pushing force is 75 N.
He pushes it for a distance of 4.0 m.

Calculate the work done by the boy in pushing the box.

....

....

3 On a building site, a crane lifts a load of bricks. The lifting force is 2500 N and the
bricks are raised to a height of 6.0 m.

a Calculate the work done by the crane in lifting the bricks.

....

b Calculate the energy that has been transferred to the bricks by the crane.

....

c Name this energy store.

....

d Explain what you notice about your answers to parts **a** and **b**.

....

4 The girl in Figure 2.7 lifts a heavy box above her head to place it on a shelf.

Figure 2.7: A girl lifting a heavy box over her head to place it on a shelf.

- Her lifting force is 120 N.
- She lifts the box to a height of 1.6 m.

a Calculate the work done by the girl in lifting the box.

....

....

b The girl decides to push the box up a sloping ramp. State and explain the factors that affect the amount of work she will do pushing the box up the slope.

....

....

....

....

c Explain why pushing the box up the slope might be preferable.

....

....

....

....

Challenge

5 We often use machines to allow us to do tasks more easily (for example, a lever to move a heavy object, or a jack to lift a car to change a tyre as in Figure 2.8). These machines allow us to use a smaller force to do the same work. By considering the conservation of energy, state and explain what else must change, when the force is reduced.

Figure 2.8: Using a jack to lift a car to change a tyre.

....

....

....

....

....

....

....

> Power

Exercise 2.8

IN THIS EXERCISE YOU WILL:

- check your understanding of the concept of power
- practise calculations involving power.

KEY WORD

watt (W): the SI unit of power; the power when 1 J of work is done in 1 s.

KEY EQUATIONS

$$\text{power} = \frac{\text{work done}}{\text{time taken}} = \frac{W}{t}$$

$$\text{power} = \frac{\text{energy transferred}}{\text{time taken}} = \frac{\Delta E}{t}$$

Focus

1   A light bulb is labelled with its power rating: 60 watt (W).

    a   How many joules of energy does it transfer in 1 s? ....

    b   How many joules of energy does it transfer in 1 minute? ....

    c   Why would it be incorrect to say that the bulb supplies 60 J of light each second?

    ....

    ....

    ....

    ....

TIP

Think of power as the rate of transfer of energy. This will stop you talking about 'power per second' for example, which makes no sense.

Remember that energy is not created, it is only transferred. Physicists get upset when you talk about creating energy.

Practice

2   A growing person needs a diet that supplies about 10 MJ of energy per day.
Calculate the amount of energy supplied by such a diet each second. (This is the
person's average power.) Give your answer to the nearest 10 W

....

....

....

....

3   A motor car is travelling at a steady speed of 30 m/s. The engine provides the force
needed to oppose the force of air resistance, 1600 N.

   a   In the space, draw a diagram to show the four forces that act on the car.

   b   Calculate the work done by the car each second against the force of
air resistance.

....

....

....

....

   c   What power is supplied by the car's engine? ....

Challenge

4 The air resistance, F_d on a car is related to the speed, v, by the formula:

$F_d = kv^2$ (This equation is not in the syllabus.)

For a certain car, the value of $k = 0.34$ and the maximum power is $317\,\text{kW}$.

a Calculate the theoretical top speed of this car.

....

....

....

b The actual top speed is $78\,\text{m/s}$. State what might account for the difference.

....

PEER ASSESSMENT

Create a set of flash cards for this chapter. Then exchange cards with another person and compare theirs to yours. Did you miss anything? Did they?

> Chapter 3

Thermal physics

> Simple kinetic particle model of matter

Exercise 3.1

IN THIS EXERCISE YOU WILL:
• check that you understand the states of matter.

Focus

1 Which states of matter are described here? Complete Table 3.1. The first example has been done for you.

Description	State or states
occupies a fixed volume	solid, liquid
evaporates to become a gas	
takes the shape of its container	
has a fixed volume	
may become a liquid when its temperature changes	

Table 3.1

> **KEY WORDS**
>
> **Brownian motion:** the motion of microscopic particles suspended in a liquid or gas, caused by molecular bombardment.
>
> **kinetic particle model of matter:** a model in which matter consists of molecules in motion.

2   Label each arrow in Figure 3.1 to show the name of the change of state.

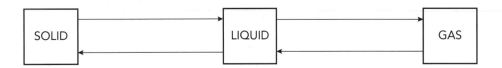

Figure 3.1: Changes of state.

3   **a**   State the temperature at which water becomes ice.

....

b   State the temperature at which water boils at standard atmospheric pressure.

....

Challenge

4   Describe and explain the changes in the molecular structure of water in the form of ice, as it is heated until the water has become steam. Consider:

   •   the arrangement of the molecules

   •   the movement of the molecules.

....

....

....

....

....

....

Exercise 3.2

IN THIS EXERCISE YOU WILL:

- check you understand the model we use to describe matter
- explain the behaviour of matter.

Focus

1   Complete the following sentences using words from the list below. Each word may be used once, more than once or not at all.

> moving   liquid   particle   gas   melt
>
> energy   faster   solid   kinetic

All substances can exist in three different states: _____,

_____ or _____. The particles that make up matter

have energy and are constantly _____. If a substance is heated, its

particles gain _____ and start to move _____.

In a _____, the particles are close together in fixed positions. In a

_____, the particles move freely but remain close together.

In a _____ the particles move freely and rapidly.

TIP

When talking about the expansion of a solid, liquid or gas, be careful *not* to talk about the particles (atoms/molecules) expanding – they don't.

2   Complete Table 3.2. In the first row, draw sketches of the three states of matter, showing the arrangement of the particles and their movement. Then describe the three states, answering the questions in the first column.

	Solid	Liquid	Gas
Sketch of particles			
How close are particles to their neighbours?			
How do the particles move?			

Table 3.2

Practice

3 **a** What word do we use to describe the process of a solid becoming a liquid?

....

b What word do we use to describe the process of a liquid becoming a gas?

....

c What word do we use to describe the process of a gas becoming a liquid?

....

4 **a** A student heated a beaker of water from room temperature of 20 °C to a temperature of 90 °C. Describe what happens to the movement of the particles.

....

b Describe what will happen to the water molecules if the student continues to heat the water.

....

....

....

Challenge

5 Why is this model of matter sometimes described as the 'kinetic particle' model?

....

....

6 A student puts an ice cube on a table in a warm classroom. When she returns later in the day, she can see no sign of the ice cube. Describe in as much detail as you can what has happened to the ice cube.

....

....

....

....

....

Exercise 3.3

Figure 3.2 shows the equipment required for observing Brownian motion. The questions in Exercise 3.3 refer to this figure.

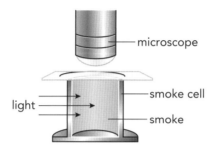

Figure 3.2: The equipment required for observing Brownian motion.

Focus

1   On Figure 3.2, show how the light coming from the left reaches the observer looking down the microscope.

2   Explain why a microscope must be used.

   ....

   ....

Practice

3   Describe briefly what the observer sees.

   ....

   ....

   ....

4   Explain why we cannot see molecules of air in the smoke cell.

   ....

   ....

Challenge

5 Explain the observations briefly using ideas from the kinetic particle model of matter.

....

....

....

....

....

> Pressure changes

Exercise 3.4

IN THIS EXERCISE YOU WILL:

- describe how the kinetic particle model explains the behaviour of gases.

KEY WORD

pressure: the force acting per unit area at right angles to a surface.

Focus

1 Figure 3.3 represents the particles of a gas inside two containers of the same size. The container on the right (B) has twice as many particles as the one on the left (A). The containers are at the same temperature.

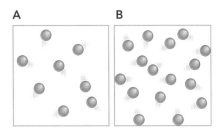

Figure 3.3: Gas particles inside two containers of the same size.

a Use diagram A in Figure 3.3 to explain why a gas exerts pressure on the walls of its container.

....

....

....

b State how the density of the gas in B compares to the density of the gas in A.

....

c Explain why the pressure of the gas in B is greater than the pressure of the gas in A.

....

....

....

d Describe how you could increase the average speed of the particles in either container.

....

....

....

Practice

2 Look at Figure 3.4. State two changes you could make to A to increase its pressure to be the same as B.

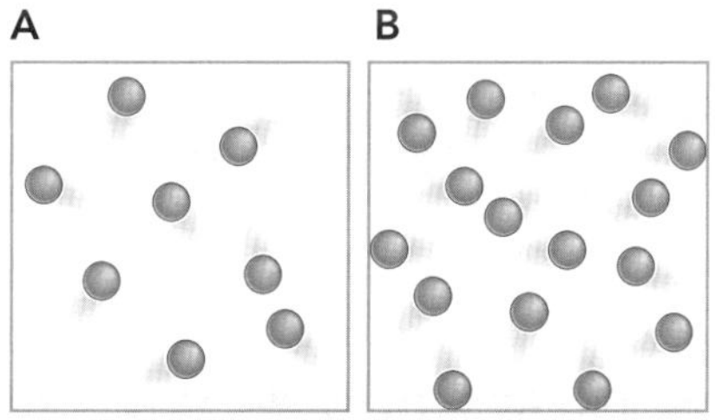

A   B

Figure 3.4: Gas particles inside two containers of the same size.

....

....

....

....

Challenge

3 A sealed container of gas is heated for a long time. After this, the gas is allowed to expand freely. State how the pressure at the end will compare to the pressure at the start. Explain your answer.

....

....

4 Explain why collisions between gas molecules and the container create pressure.

....

....

....

....

5 Explain why increasing the temperature of a gas increases the pressure it exerts.

....

....

....

....

> Matter and thermal properties
Exercise 3.5

IN THIS EXERCISE YOU WILL:
• describe an experiment to observe thermal expansion
• describe some uses and problems relating to thermal expansion.

KEY WORDS

thermal expansion: the expansion of a material when its temperature rises.

Focus

1 Complete the following sentences to describe thermal expansion.

When a substance is _____, it will expand.

When the substance is _____, it will contract.

This behaviour is called _____ and it happens in solids, liquids and gases.

2 The 'bar-and-gauge' experiment is often used to show that a metal expands when heated (see Figure 3.5).

TIP

It is difficult to see the expansion of a metal even when it is heated by several hundred degrees. However, experiments and practical examples make it very clear.

Figure 3.5: The bar and gauge apparatus can be used to show thermal expansion.

Write step-by-step instructions for a teacher who wants to use this demonstration of thermal expansion and who also wants to show that metals contract on cooling. Include practical instructions.

....

....

....

....

....

....

Practice

3 **a** Give an example of a problem that can occur when a solid expands on a hot day.

....

....

....

b An alcohol-in-glass thermometer is used to measure temperatures in the laboratory. Explain why the liquid moves up the tube when the bulb of the thermometer is placed in boiling water.

....

....

....

c   Explain why the liquid moves back down the tube when the bulb is removed from the boiling water.

....

....

....

Challenge

4   A bimetallic strip is made of strips of steel and invar, riveted together. In the space below, draw such a strip and indicate how it will bend if it is heated. (Steel expands more than invar when it is heated.)

....

....

....

5   Table 3.3 shows the 'volume coefficient of expansivity' for several materials. This tells us the fraction by which a material's volume will increase for a 1 °C rise in temperature.

Material	Expansivity per °C (all × 10^{-6})
air	3400
water	207
gasoline (petrol)	950
iron, carbon steel	33
Pyrex glass	10
invar (a metal alloy)	3.6
copper	51
concrete	36
brass	57
PVC (a polymer)	156

Table 3.3

Use data from Table 3.3 to answer the following questions.

a   Which material expands the most? ....

b   Which material expands the least? ....

c   Which liquid expands the most? ....

d   Which non-metallic solid expands the least? ....

e   Why would it not be satisfactory to make a bimetallic strip
    from copper and brass?

    ....

    ....

f   Suggest a better pair of metals from which to make a bimetallic strip.

    ....

〉 Thermal processes

Exercise 3.6

IN THIS EXERCISE YOU WILL:
• list examples of conductors and insulators
• describe experiments to test which materials are good conductors and which are good insulators
• check your understanding of why some materials are good thermal (and electrical) conductors.

KEY WORDS

conduction: the transfer of thermal energy or electricity through a material without movement of the material itself.

conductor: a substance that transmits thermal energy.

convection: the transfer of thermal energy through a material by movement of the material itself.

Focus

1   Complete the following sentences to explain how thermal energy is transferred by conduction.

The particles in a _____ cannot move freely. They vibrate about fixed positions.

If one end of the solid is heated, the particles at that end vibrate

_____ and this is passed on to neighbouring particles.

As the vibrations are passed through the solid, so is _____ energy.

This method of thermal energy transfer is called _____ and it happens best in solids. It does not happen much in _____ or _____.

Substances which transfer thermal energy in this way are called _____.

2 **a** Copper is an example of a good conductor of thermal energy. What word is the opposite of 'conductor'?

....

   b Give another example of a good conductor of thermal energy.

....

   c Give an example of a poor conductor of thermal energy.

....

3 Place each of these materials in the correct column in Table 3.4.

copper   **glass**   **plastic**   **gold**   **wood**   **air**   **iron**

Thermal conductors	Thermal insulators

Table 3.4

4 State what metals have, that non-metals generally do not have, which allows them to conduct heat and electricity.

....

> **KEY WORDS**
>
> **electromagnetic radiation:** energy travelling in the form of waves.
>
> **infrared radiation:** electromagnetic radiation whose wavelength is greater than that of visible light; sometimes known as thermal radiation.
>
> **insulator:** a substance that transmits thermal energy very poorly.

Practice

5 Figure 3.6 shows an experiment used to compare the conductivity of different metals.

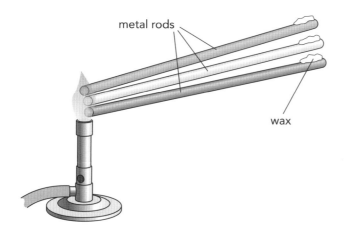

Figure 3.6: Three rods of different metals, with one end of each rod being heated. There is solid wax on the other end of each rod.

a State *two* things that must be the same for all three rods, to make this a fair test.

....

....

b Explain how you can tell which metal is the best conductor, and which is the worst.

....

....

....

6 A pan is made from aluminium, with a copper base. Its handle is made of plastic. Explain why these materials were chosen by the person who designed the pan.

....

....

....

....

7 Metals are usually good conductors of both thermal energy and electricity. Explain why this is.

....

....

....

....

Challenge

8 Explain why liquids and gases are poor conductors of thermal energy.

....

....

....

Exercise 3.7

IN THIS EXERCISE YOU WILL:

- check that you recall and understand what convection is
- describe how convection works
- describe practical implications of convection as thermal energy transfer.

Focus

1 Complete the following sentences to explain how thermal energy is transferred by convection.

When a fluid (a _____ or _____) is heated it becomes less

dense, so it is lighter than the cold fluid around it. This causes _____

fluids to rise and _____ fluids to sink. This method of transferring

thermal energy throughout the fluid is called _____. This method of

thermal energy transfer cannot happen in _____.

Practice

2 **a** Figure 3.7 shows a room with a heater next to one wall, opposite a window. Draw on the figure to show how a convection current will form in the room when the heater is switched on.

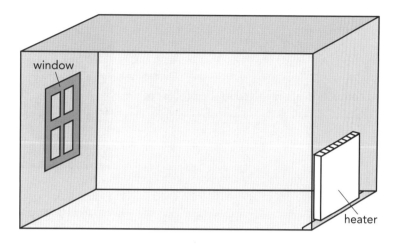

Figure 3.7: A room with a heater next to one wall, opposite a window.

b Explain, in terms of convection, why it would not be sensible to fix the heater high up on the wall, close to the ceiling.

....

....

....

3 How do the following quantities change when air is heated? Choose from:

increases   **decreases**   **stays the same**

a Temperature ....

b Mass..

c Density...

d Separation of molecules ....

e Speed of molecules...

Challenge

4   Figure 3.8 shows a gas cooker being used to heat water.

   a   Describe the energy transfer which takes place as the gas is burned.

   ....

   ....

   ....

   b   Describe how both conduction and convection are involved in the process of heating the water.

   ....

   ....

   ....

   ....

Figure 3.8:
A pan of boiling water.

5   Explain in detail why the smoke produced by a candle flame rises upwards.

   ....

   ....

   ....

   ....

   ....

   ....

Exercise 3.8

IN THIS EXERCISE YOU WILL:

- check your understanding of what infrared radiation is

- explain how different surfaces emit, absorb and reflect infrared radiation, and describe practical implications of this mechanism of thermal energy transfer

- check your understanding of the different factors affecting the rate of transfer of infrared radiation.

Focus

1 Complete the following sentences to describe thermal energy transfer by radiation.

Thermal energy can be transferred by waves. These waves are called

_____ radiation. They are part of a large group of waves called

the _____ spectrum.

The waves can travel through a _____ and so this is the method
by which thermal energy is transferred from the Sun to the Earth.

The amount of thermal radiation absorbed or emitted by an object depends on its

surface. Dull, _____ surfaces are good absorbers and emitters.

_____, _____ surfaces are poor absorbers

and emitters.

> **TIP**
>
> In physics, we talk about two kinds of radiation – ionising and non-ionising. Most of the electromagnetic spectrum is not ionising – the exceptions are X-rays and gamma rays. Nuclear radiation is ionising. Make sure you are clear on the difference.

2 Two identical cups containing equal volumes of water sit on a table.
One starts at a temperature of 50 °C. The other starts at a temperature of 40 °C.
State which will cool more quickly. Explain your answer.

....

....

....

....

....

Practice

3 Explain why energy from the Sun can reach us by radiation but not by conduction
or convection.

....

....

....

4 Infrared radiation may be absorbed when it reaches the surface of an object.
Describe the surface of an object that is a good absorber of infrared radiation.

....

....

5   What effect does infrared radiation have on an object that absorbs it?

....

....

6   A cold object and a warm object are in the same room at the same time.
    Explain why the cold object will warm up and the warm object will cool down,
    in terms of exchange of infrared radiation.

....

....

....

7   An ice cube is taken from the freezer. Its temperature will increase at first but
    when it reaches room temperature, it will remain at this temperature. Explain why
    this happens.

....

....

....

Challenge

8   In cold countries, windows are often fitted with double glazing. This consists of
    two sheets of glass separated by a gap a few millimetres wide. There is usually a
    vacuum in the gap.

    a   Explain why very little energy escapes from a room by conduction through
        double-glazed windows.

        ....

        ....

        ....

    b   Explain why very little energy escapes from a room by convection through
        double-glazed windows.

        ....

        ....

        ....

> TIP
>
> Insulation is all about reducing thermal energy transfer. We cannot stop this energy transfer, so don't be tempted to say 'insulation stops heat loss'.
>
> To be as effective as possible, we needs to consider every means of thermal energy transfer.
>
> Remember, if something stops thermal energy leaving, it will also stop thermal energy getting in.

c   Can energy escape by radiation? Explain your answer.

....

....

....

9   A television remote control uses infrared radiation to send instructions to the TV set. If you point it in the opposite direction, the beam misses the TV set and nothing happens.

However, infrared radiation can be reflected by hard, shiny surfaces such as glass or aluminium. In the space below, draw a diagram to show how you could use a remote control, a TV set and a sheet of aluminium to show the reflection of infrared radiation.

Try this at home: Although our eyes cannot see infrared radiation, a digital camera may detect it. Try shining a TV remote control into a digital camera (the camera on a mobile phone will work). Notice that the camera detects the infrared radiation from the TV remote control.

10 The heat sink around the processor in a computer is often a piece of aluminium. It is needed to remove thermal energy from the processor while the processor is in operation. This allows the processor to remain cool enough to function properly. State and explain *two* design features that would make the heat sink an effective emitter of thermal radiation.

....

....

....

....

....

11 Explain why gases such as carbon dioxide and methane contribute to global warming.

....

....

....

....

....

Exercise 3.9

IN THIS EXERCISE YOU WILL:

- identify and explain some consequences and applications of thermal energy transfer

- check that you understand experimental technique, in the context of thermal energy transfer

- explain how a vacuum flask works.

Focus

1 The examples in Table 3.5 describe situations where thermal energy is transferred. For each example, state which type of thermal energy transfer is involved and explain what is happening.

Example	Type of thermal energy transfer (conduction, convection or radiation)	Explanation
A girl wearing a black T-shirt gets very hot, while her friend wearing a white T-shirt keeps cool.		
The element of a kettle is at the bottom.		
The handle of an iron is made of plastic but the part used to iron the clothes is metal.		

Table 3.5

2   Figure 3.9 shows an experiment to investigate the loss of energy from a beaker of
    hot water. Beaker A has a plastic lid; beaker B has no lid.

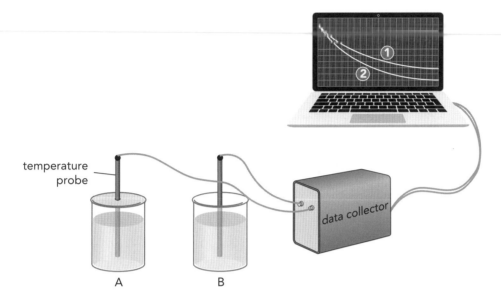

temperature
probe

Figure 3.9: An experiment to investigate the loss of energy from a beaker of hot water,
with and without a lid.

At the start of the experiment, both beakers are filled with hot water from a kettle.
The temperature sensors record the changing temperature of the water in
each beaker.

a   State *one* quantity that should be the same for each beaker if this is to be a
    fair test.

    ....

b   State *one* other factor that should be controlled if this is to be a fair test.

    ....

c   State which graph line (1 or 2) on the computer in Figure 3.9 is for beaker A.

    ....

d   Explain your answer.

    ....

Practice

3 A learner suggests that beaker B in Figure 3.9 is losing energy by convection. State one other way it could be losing energy.

....

4 Explain why the test would have been better if the beakers had been insulated around their sides and bases.

....

....

....

....

....

Challenge

5 Figure 3.10 shows a vacuum flask, which is very good at reducing the transfer of thermal energy into or out of the contents. Complete Table 3.6, using your knowledge of the ways in which thermal energy transfer occurs.

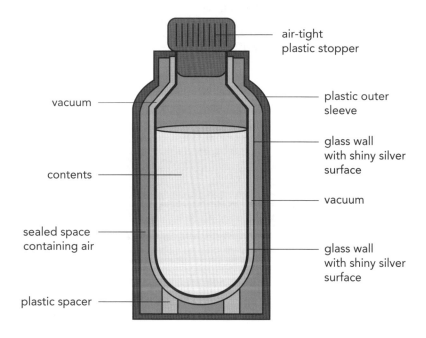

Figure 3.10: The structure of a vacuum flask.

Thermal energy transfer mechanism	Parts of the flask which reduce this type of thermal energy transfer	Explanation
conduction		
convection		
infrared radiation		

Table 3.6

Exercise 3.10

IN THIS EXERCISE YOU WILL:

- apply your knowledge to the Earth and how it gains and loses thermal energy.

Focus

The Earth is a giant rock in space. It is about 150 million kilometres from the Sun. It is daytime on the side of the Earth facing the Sun. It is night-time on the other side (see Figure 3.11).

Sun   Earth

Figure 3.11: The relative positions of the Earth and the Sun, and where day and night are on the Earth as a result.

The Earth's average temperature is about 15 °C. The Earth is in space. Space is very cold – its temperature is about −270 °C. Because the Earth is warmer than space, it is constantly losing energy into space.

1 State how the Earth transfers energy into space: by conduction, by convection or by radiation.

....

2 Describe what would happen to the temperature of the Earth if the Sun stopped shining.

....

....

3 Fortunately, the Sun shines at an almost steady rate. The side of the Earth facing the Sun absorbs the Sun's radiation.

Explain what happens to the temperature of the Earth on the side facing the Sun.

....

....

Practice

4 Explain why the temperature of the Earth usually falls at night.

....

....

....

5 Because the Earth spins on its axis, the night ends and a new day begins. The graph in Figure 3.12 shows how the temperature at one point on the Earth varies during a week.

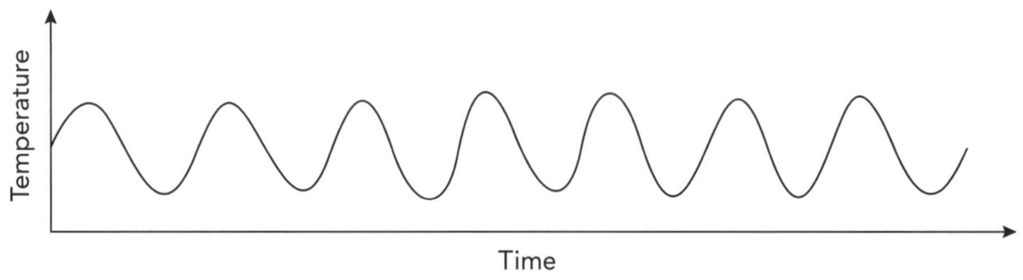

Figure 3.12: Graph of the variation of temperature at a point on the Earth's surface over the period of one week.

Explain why the lowest temperature is often just before dawn.

....

....

Challenge

6   Imagine that the Earth turned more slowly, so that a day lasted twice as long: 48 hours. Think about temperatures during the day and at night. Describe the changes that we would notice. Explain your answer. On the graph grid below, draw a graph similar to the one in Figure 3.12 to illustrate your answer.

....

....

....

....

Chapter 4

Properties of waves

> General wave properties

Exercise 4.1

IN THIS EXERCISE YOU WILL:

- recall that a wave transfers energy from place to place without any matter being transferred
- practise your understanding of wave motion
- recall key words for describing the properties of waves.

KEY EQUATION

wave speed = frequency × wavelength

$$v = f\lambda$$

Focus

1 Figure 4.1 represents a wave.

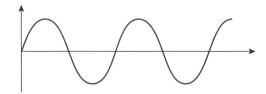

Figure 4.1: A wave on a string.

On Figure 4.1, add the labels 'crest' and 'trough' in the correct places.

2 Waves can be described as transverse or longitudinal.

a State in which type of wave the vibrations are at right angles to the direction in which the wave is travelling. ....

b State which type of wave a sound wave is. ....

c State which type of wave a light wave is. ....

KEY WORDS

amplitude: the greatest height of a wave above its undisturbed level.

crest/peak: the highest point of a wave.

diffraction: the spreading out of a wave as it passes through a gap.

frequency: the number of vibrations per second or waves per second passing a point.

Hertz: the unit of frequency; 1 Hz = 1 wave per second.

longitudinal wave: a wave in which the vibration is forward and back, along the direction in which the wave is travelling.

reflection: the change in direction of a ray of light or a wave when it strikes a surface without passing through it.

Practice

3 Figure 4.2 shows a wave on a string. Complete the sentences below to describe the wave.

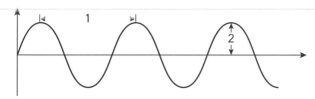

Figure 4.2: A wave in a string.

The wave transfers _____ .

The distance labelled 1 is the _____ of the wave. The symbol

for this is _____ and the unit is _____ .

The distance labelled 2 is the _____ of the wave.

4 Complete Table 4.1 by classifying each of the following waves as transverse or longitudinal.

Wave	Transverse or longitudinal?
Water waves	
Sound waves	
Light waves	
Seismic P waves	
Seismic S waves	
Electromagnetic waves	

Table 4.1

Challenge

5 Describe which property of a sound wave changes when a sound gets louder.

....

....

6 You have a long spring stretched out in front of you on a long table.
Another learner holds the far end so it cannot move.

a Describe how you should move your end of the spring to produce a transverse wave.

....

....

b Describe how you should move your end of the spring to produce a longitudinal wave.

....

....

Exercise 4.2

IN THIS EXERCISE YOU WILL:

- practise calculating the speed of a wave crest as the wave travels along

- use the wave equation $v = f\lambda$ to show how wave speed (v) is related to frequency (f) and wavelength (λ).

Focus

1 Complete Table 4.2 to show the quantities related by the equation $v = f\lambda$ and their units.

Symbol	Quantity	Unit (name and symbol)
v		
f		
λ		

Table 4.2

> **TIP**
>
> In these calculations, you may need to convert units. Make sure you know the meanings of prefixes such as m (milli = 0.001), k (kilo = 1000) and M (mega = 1 000 000).

2 A particular sound wave has a frequency of 100 Hz.

a State how many waves pass a point in 1 s. ....

b Each wave has a wavelength of 3.3 m. Calculate the total length of the waves

that pass a point in 1 s. ....

c Calculate the speed of the sound wave. ....

Practice

3   Seismic waves are caused by earthquakes. They travel out from the affected area and can be detected around the world. They have low frequencies (mostly too low to hear).

a   A particular seismic wave is travelling through granite at a speed of 5000 m/s. Its frequency is 8.0 Hz. Calculate its wavelength.

....

....

....

b   The wave is detected 12.5 minutes after the earthquake. Estimate the distance from the detector to the site of the earthquake.

....

....

....

Challenge

4   **a**   Light travels at a speed of 3.0×10^8 m/s. Red light has a wavelength of 7.0×10^{-7} m. Calculate its frequency.

....

....

b   Infrared radiation travels at the same speed as light but it has a lower frequency than red light. State whether its wavelength is greater than or less than that of red light.

....

Exercise 4.3

Focus

1 Complete Table 4.3 to show the names of these aspects of waves.

Description	Name
Bouncing off a surface	
Changing direction because of a change of speed	
Spreading out after passing through a gap	

Table 4.3

> **TIP**
>
> Each word ends in …tion.

Practice

2 Figure 4.3 shows light waves travelling through two different materials, 1 and 2.

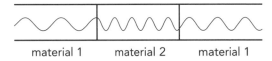

material 1   material 2   material 1

Figure 4.3: Ray diagram of a light wave travelling through two different materials.

Complete Table 4.4 to show how the speed, wavelength and frequency of the waves change as they travel from material 1 into material 2.

Quantity	Increases / decreases / stays the same
Wave speed	
Wavelength	
Frequency	

Table 4.4

Challenge

3 It is possible to hear a conversation through a partially open door, but not to see the people talking. Explain this using the idea of diffraction.

....

....

....

....

....

....

> Light

Exercise 4.4

IN THIS EXERCISE YOU WILL:

- practise drawing ray diagrams
- use the law of reflection
- check your understanding of real and virtual images.

KEY EQUATIONS

angle of incidence = angle of reflection; $i = r$

$$\text{refractive index} = \frac{\text{sin angle of incidence}}{\text{sin angle of refraction}}$$

$$n = \frac{\sin i}{\sin r}$$

KEY WORDS

angle of incidence: the angle between the incident ray and the normal.

angle of reflection: the angle between the reflected ray and the normal.

angle of refraction: the angle between the refracted ray and the normal.

converging lens: rays that enter a converging lens parallel to the principal axis pass through the principal focus after leaving the lens; these lenses usually form real images.

Focus

1 a State where the image created by a plane mirror is formed.

....

b State the property of the reflected image that means an image cannot be formed on a screen.

....

c A ray of light makes an angle of 22° with a plane mirror. Calculate its angle of reflection. State the relationship that allows you to say what the angle will be.

....

2 In the space below, draw a diagram to show the path of the ray in question **1c**. Mark the angle of incidence and the angle of reflection.

Practice

3 The incomplete ray diagram in Figure 4.4 shows an object in front of a plane mirror. Three light rays are shown leaving the object.

a Follow the instructions to complete Figure 4.4.

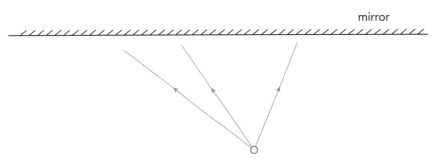

Figure 4.4: An incomplete ray diagram for an object in front of a plane mirror.

- Extend the rays to the mirror.
- For each ray, use a ruler and protractor to draw the reflected rays.
- Extend the reflected rays to find where they meet.
- Mark the position of the image.
- Measure the distance from the image to the mirror.

b State the distance of the image from the mirror. ....

c Is this image real or virtual? ....

d Explain your answer to part c.

....

....

Challenge

4 Figure 4.5 shows a ray of light incident on a pair of mirrors.

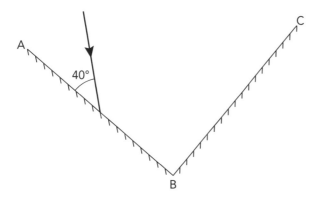

Figure 4.5: A ray of light striking two plane mirrors at right angles to each other.

a On Figure 4.5, draw the path of the light as it reflects from mirror AB.

b On Figure 4.5, draw the path of the light as it reflects from mirror BC.

c Complete this sentence. The incident and final reflected rays are

....

Exercise 4.5

IN THIS EXERCISE YOU WILL:

- complete a diagram to show that a ray of light is refracted when it passes from one transparent material to another

- explain how light behaves when it is refracted.

Focus

1   Define the word *refraction*.

    ....

Practice

2   State what happens to a ray of light as it passes:

    a   from air to glass

        ....

    b   from glass to air.

        ....

Challenge

3   Figure 4.6 shows a ray of light travelling from air into glass.

    a   Follow the instructions to complete the figure.

        - Label the materials 'air' and 'glass'.

        - Add arrows to the rays to show the direction in which the light is travelling.

        - Using a ruler, draw the normal to the surface at the point where the ray enters the glass.

        - Add labels 'incident ray' and 'refracted ray'.

        - Using a protractor, measure the angles of incidence and refraction.

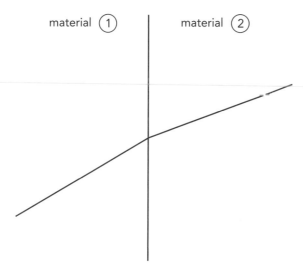

Figure 4.6: A ray of light travelling from air into glass.

b Explain how you know which material is air and which is glass.

....

....

....

c State the angle of incidence. ....

d State the angle of refraction. ....

Exercise 4.6

IN THIS EXERCISE YOU WILL:

- explain that light travels at different speeds in different materials and this is what causes refraction

- practise calculating refractive index.

Focus

1 The refractive index of a certain material is 1.45. State whether light travels more quickly or more slowly in this material than in air.

....

2   A ray of light passes through the material in question **1**. As it leaves the material, state whether it will bend towards or away from the normal.

....

Practice

3   A ray of light passing through air enters a block of Perspex. Its angle of incidence is 30°.

a   In the space below, draw a diagram of the ray of light passing through the glass block, showing the angles of incidence and refraction.

b   The refractive index of Perspex is 1.50. Calculate the angle of refraction of the light as it enters the block.

....

4   Describe an experiment to measure the angle of refraction for light travelling from air into a rectangular glass block.

....

....

....

....

....

....

....

....

Challenge

5   Explain, using Figure 4.7, why a swimming pool does not look as deep as it actually is.

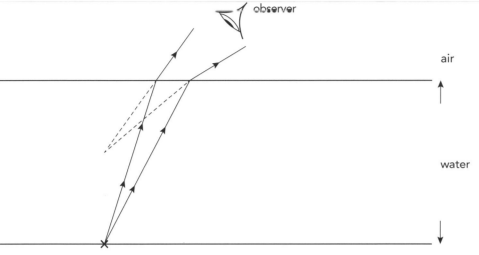

Figure 4.7: The paths of two rays of light coming from the bottom of a swimming pool and leaving the water.

....

....

....

PEER ASSESSMENT

Pair up with a partner and discuss your answers. Try to agree on them! Present your answers to the class, pair by pair.

Exercise 4.7

IN THIS EXERCISE YOU WILL:

- recall what happens when light is reflected in the process of total internal reflection
- explain the significance of the critical angle
- describe applications of total internal reflection in the real world.

Focus

1   Triangular prisms are often used as perfect mirrors in periscopes, telescopes and binoculars. Figure 4.8 shows how a light ray is reflected by a prism (the angles of the prism are 90°, 45°, 45°).

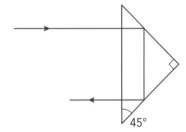

Figure 4.8: How light is totally internally reflected in a triangular prism.

  a   On Figure 4.8, mark with an X two points at which the light ray undergoes total internal reflection.

  b   State the angle of incidence of the ray at this point. ....

Practice

2   Explain why the ray in Figure 4.8 does not bend at the point where it enters the prism, or where it leaves the prism.

....

....

....

Challenge

3 Figure 4.9 shows a periscope that makes use of two prisms.

a Complete the figure by extending the two rays until they reach the observer.

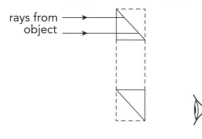

Figure 4.9: Two triangular prisms, like the one in Figure 4.8, used to make a periscope.

b Explain how you can tell from Figure 4.9 that the image seen by the observer will be the right way up, rather than inverted.

....

....

....

....

4 Figure 4.10 shows light travelling down an optical fibre. Explain, using the figure, why it is important that these fibres are not bent too much.

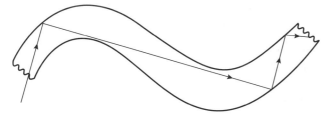

Figure 4.10: A ray of light passing through an optical fibre.

....

....

....

....

Exercise 4.8

TIP

Converging lenses are everywhere – in cameras, in telescopes, in our eyes. A converging lens collects rays of light and focuses them to form an image. Check that you understand the rules for drawing ray diagrams.

IN THIS EXERCISE YOU WILL:

- explain your understanding of lenses

- draw ray diagrams for real images formed by lenses

- describe real-world applications of lenses.

Focus

1   Figure 4.11 shows an incomplete ray diagram – no rays have been drawn yet! There is an object O to the left of the lens.

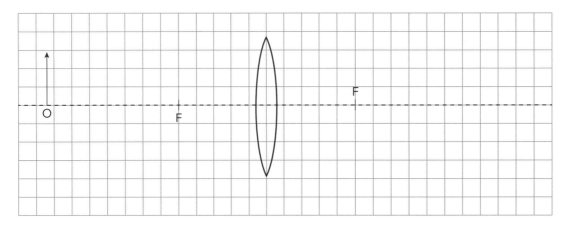

Figure 4.11: An incomplete ray diagram showing an object (O) at a distance greater than twice the focal length of the lens.

a   State the name of the dotted line through the centre of the lens. ....

b   State what the letter F indicates. ....

Practice

2   a   Complete the ray diagram in Figure 4.11 by following the instructions.

- Draw one ray from the top of the object, passing through the centre of the lens.

- Draw a second ray from the top of the object, that is initially parallel to the principal axis of the lens.

- Indicate where the image of the object is formed.

b   State which is bigger, the object or the image. ....

c   State which is further from the lens, the object or the image. ....

d   State whether the image is upright or inverted. ....

3   You can use a ray diagram as a scale drawing.

a   The focal length of the lens is 10.0 cm. State how far the image is from the

centre of the lens. ....

b   The object is 6.0 mm tall. State the size of the image. ....

Challenge

4   When a converging lens is used as a magnifying glass, the object O (marked on the diagram below) must be closer to the lens than F, the focal length.

a   Complete the ray diagram in Figure 4.12 to show where the image of O will be formed.

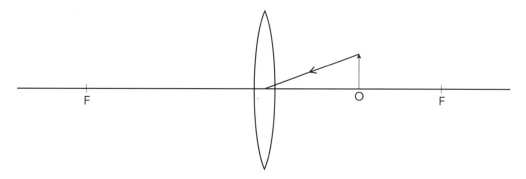

Figure 4.12: A ray diagram showing an object (O) at a distance less than the focal length of the lens.

b   State whether the image is upright or inverted. ....

c   State whether the image is real or virtual. ....

d   Explain how you can tell from the diagram that the image is magnified.

....

....

Exercise 4.9

IN THIS EXERCISE YOU WILL:

• recall key facts about light waves and the visible spectrum.

Focus

1 The visible spectrum is the spectrum of all the colours of light that we can see.

   a State which colour in the visible spectrum has the shortest wavelength.

    ....

   b State which colour in the visible spectrum has the highest frequency.

    ....

   c State which colour comes between green and indigo. ....

   d State which colour has a wavelength longer than orange light. ....

Practice

2 Figure 4.13 shows a ray of white light hitting a prism. Complete the figure to show what happens to the light. Either use colour or label the colours produced.

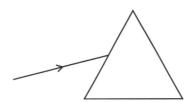

Figure 4.13: A ray of white light hitting a triangular prism.

Challenge

3 Figure 4.14 represents two waves of visible light, observed for a tiny fraction of a second.

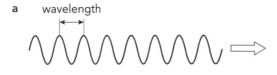

Figure 4.14: Two waves of visible light, observed for a tiny fraction of a second.

a   State which wave (A or B) has the greater wavelength. ....

b   State how many complete waves there are in trace A. ....

c   State how many complete waves there are in trace B. ....

d   Explain how you know that the waves are travelling at the same speed.

....

....

e   State which wave represents light of a higher frequency. ....

f   The waves represent red and violet light. State which one represents red light.

....

> The electromagnetic spectrum

Exercise 4.10

IN THIS EXERCISE YOU WILL:

- describe the uses of regions of the electromagnetic spectrum
- practise extended writing in the context of the electromagnetic spectrum
- explain how electromagnetic waves have many different uses.

KEY WORDS

electromagnetic spectrum: a range of electromagnetic waves with different wavelengths which travel at the same speed (the speed of light) and can travel through a vacuum.

infrared radiation: electromagnetic radiation whose wavelength is greater than that of visible light; sometimes known as thermal radiation.

Focus

1   The electromagnetic spectrum is the spectrum of all types of electromagnetic radiation, arranged according to their frequencies.

a   State which type of electromagnetic radiation has the highest frequency.

....

b   State which type of electromagnetic radiation has the longest wavelength.

....

c   State which type of electromagnetic radiation has a frequency just greater than that of visible light. ....

d   State which type of electromagnetic radiation has the most damaging effects on the human body. ....

Practice

2 The list on the left shows different types of electromagnetic radiation. The list on the right shows uses of the types of radiation. The lists are not in order.

Draw lines to link each type of electromagnetic radiation with the correct use. There is one use for each type of radiation.

Electromagnetic radiation	Radiation use
gamma rays	eyesight
X-rays	transmitting TV programmes
ultraviolet	airport baggage scanners
visible light	grilling food
infrared	sterilising medical equipment
microwaves	communicating with spacecraft
radio waves	forgery detection (banknotes)

KEY WORDS

spectrum: waves, or colours of light, separated out in order according to their wavelengths.

ultraviolet radiation: electromagnetic radiation whose frequency is higher than that of visible light.

TIP

The electromagnetic spectrum includes ALL the waves coming from the Sun. It is continuous – there are no gaps between the different parts of the spectrum. For example, radio waves are just like long wavelength microwaves. We split up the spectrum according to the amount of energy delivered by the different types of radiation.

Challenge

3 Some electromagnetic waves can be dangerous. For each of the following waves, state the hazard and describe precautions which can be taken to minimise the hazard

a Ultraviolet radiation

Hazard...

Precautions..

....

b X-rays

Hazard...

Precautions..

....

Create a set of flash cards of the electromagnetic spectrum. You might do this on paper or use a free online program. In your flash cards, you should include:

a   the direction of increasing frequency

b   the direction of decreasing wavelength

c   the order of the colours of visible light within the overall electromagnetic spectrum

d   uses of each member of the spectrum.

Now share your flash cards with others while you use theirs. Compare your sets and feed back to the author of the other sets:

- What did you like?

- How could they improve their flashcards?

- Were there any errors?

〉 Sound

Exercise 4.11

IN THIS EXERCISE YOU WILL:

- check that you understand how sound is made

- practise remembering the normal human hearing range

- practise measuring the speed of sound

- use the wave equation.

KEY WORDS

amplitude: the greatest height of a wave above its undisturbed level.

frequency: the number of vibrations per second or the number of waves per second passing a point.

period: the time for one complete vibration or the passage of one complete wave.

pitch: how high or low a note sounds.

Focus

1   **a**   State the *one* word that describes the movement of a source of sound.

....

b   State which part of a guitar moves to produce a sound.

....

c   State what moves when a wind instrument such as a flute produces a sound.

....

d   State what we call a reflected sound.

....

2 State the normal hearing range for humans.

....

Practice

3 Arun can hear sounds with frequencies up to 20 kHz. His grandfather cannot hear sounds above 12 kHz.

Which *two* of the following sound frequencies will Arun hear but his grandfather will not?

      8.0 kHz   **25.2 kHz**   **16.5 kHz**   **14.9 kHz**   **11.8 kHz**

....

4 **a** The speed of sound in air is 330 m/s. Calculate how long a sound will take to travel 1 km in air. Give your answer in seconds, to one decimal place.

....

....

....

    b Calculate how far sound will travel in 5 s in air.

....

....

5 Figure 4.15 shows a method for determining the speed of sound.

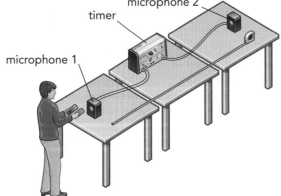

Figure 4.15: A method for calculating the speed of sound.

Complete the following sentences:

a   This experiment measures the speed of sound in ....

b   To make a sound, ...

c   The microphones detect the sound and the timer shows

....

d   The boy must also measure ....

e   The formula for calculating the speed of sound from this experiment is

....

TIP

Make sure you know how to convert between units milliseconds to seconds, kilometres to metres, etc. – as they are common in this section.

Challenge

6   In an experiment to measure the speed of sound in glass, a pulse of sound is sent into a glass rod that is 14.0 m long. The reflected sound is detected after 5.6 ms (0.0056 s). Calculate the speed of sound in glass.

....

....

....

Exercise 4.12

IN THIS EXERCISE YOU WILL:

• explain how to use some laboratory equipment to make measurements for sound waves

• relate the shape of a sound wave to the sound we hear.

Focus

1   Can sound waves travel through a vacuum (empty space)? ....

2   a   State what instrument we use to detect sound waves in the school laboratory.

....

b   State what instrument we use to display sound waves on a screen.

....

3   Complete the following sentences, using words from the list below. Each word may be used once, more than once, or not at all:

wavelength   cm³   metres   hertz   pressure

5000 Hz   20 000 Hz   amplitude   frequency

The _____ of a wave is the number of waves each second. This can

be measured in _____ It tells us about the pitch of the sound.

The highest pitch humans can hear is _____ .

The _____ of a sound tells us how loud it is. This can be measured

in _____ .

Practice

4   Figure 4.16 shows a trace that represents a sound wave. Draw a second wave on the figure that has the same pitch but is louder.

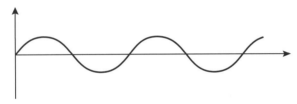

Figure 4.16: A trace representing a sound wave.

5   Two sound waves have the frequencies shown:

- sound A, 440 Hz
- sound B, 520 Hz.

State which sound has the higher pitch. ....

Challenge

6   Complete the following sentences, using words from the list below. Each word may be used once, more than once, or not at all.

compressions   longitudinal   high   transverse   rarefactions

low   electromagnetic   peaks   atmospheric   troughs

Sound waves are _____ waves.
They consist of:

- _____, which are _____ pressure areas

- _____, which are _____ pressure areas.

Chapter 5

Electricity and magnetism

> Simple phenomena of magnetism

Exercise 5.1

IN THIS EXERCISE YOU WILL:

- check your understanding of what a magnet is
- describe how to distinguish between a magnet and a magnetic material
- describe the attractive and repulsive forces between magnets
- describe the field around a bar magnet
- recall that magnetic field lines are used to represent the shape of a magnetic field.

KEY WORDS

electromagnet: a coil of wire that becomes a magnet when a current flows in it. An electromagnet can be turned on or off. The strength of an electromagnet depends on the size of the current flowing through the coil of wire (the solenoid).

hard magnetic material: a material that, once magnetised, is difficult to demagnetise; steel is a hard magnetic material.

magnet: a device which exerts a force on magnetic materials.

magnetisation: causing a piece of material to be magnetised; a material is magnetised when it produces a magnetic field around itself.

Focus

1   Figure 5.1 shows two bar magnets. One pole has been labelled. The two magnets are repelling each other.

Figure 5.1: Two bar magnets repelling each other.

   a On Figure 5.1, label the other three poles in such a way that the magnets will repel each other.

   b On Figure 5.1, draw force arrows to show the magnetic force on each magnet.

2   In Figure 5.2, the two bar magnets are attracting each other.

Figure 5.2: Two bar magnets attracting each other.

On Figure 5.2, label the four poles and draw force arrows to show the magnetic force on each magnet.

3 Figure 5.3 shows a bar magnet. On Figure 5.3, draw the magnetic field around the magnet.

Figure 5.3: A bar magnet.

Practice

4 Describe a method that you can use to find the shape of the magnetic field around a bar magnet. Your method should include how you can determine the direction of the field lines.

....

....

5 Figure 5.4 shows a horseshoe-shaped permanent magnet attracting a steel rod. The attraction shows that magnetic poles are induced in the rod.

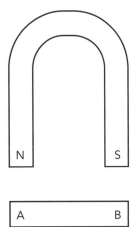

Figure 5.4: A permanent horseshoe magnet attracting a steel rod.

KEY WORDS

magnetic field: the region of space around a magnet or electric current in which a magnet will feel a force.

magnetic field line: a line showing the force exerted by a magnetic field; the direction of a magnetic field line at a point in a magnetic field is the direction of the force on a north pole placed at that point.

magnetic material: a material on which a magnet exerts a force and which can be magnetised; common magnetic materials are iron, steel, nickel, cobalt.

soft magnetic material: a material that, once magnetised, is easily demagnetised; soft iron is a soft magnetic material.

solenoid: a long narrow coil of wire.

a   State and explain what type of pole (N or S) must be induced in end A of the rod.

....

....

b   State what type of pole (N or S) must be induced in end B of the rod.

....

Challenge

6   A student is given three metal bars and a plotting compass. One bar is steel, one is aluminium and one is a magnet. Describe what the student should do to identify which bar is which.

....

....

....

Exercise 5.2

IN THIS EXERCISE YOU WILL:

*   check your understanding of the differences between permanent magnets and electromagnets and their uses.

Focus

1   Describe the differences between a permanent magnet and an electromagnet.

....

....

....

....

....

....

....

TIP

Consider each atom of a magnetic material as a little magnet.

Before the material is magnetised, these 'atomic' magnets point in random directions.

Magnetising the material is the process of causing these 'atomic' magnets to line up, so they point in the same direction. The more that line up, the stronger the magnetic field around the material.

Demagnetising is the reverse of this; it causes the arrangement to be random again. A material can be demagnetised by shock (e.g. hitting it with a hammer), heating or applying another magnetic field.

2   Draw the magnetic field around the electromagnet in Figure 5.5.

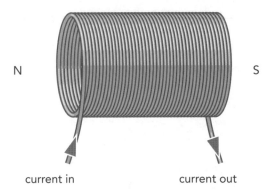

N   S

current in   current out

Figure 5.5: An electromagnet.

Practice

3   Explain whether you would use soft iron or steel for an electromagnet.

    ....

    ....

4   Describe a method by which you could determine the polarity of an electromagnet.

    ....

    ....

    ....

    ....

Challenge

5   A student accidentally got iron filings in her eye. When she went to hospital,
    the doctor used a very strong magnet to remove the metal. State whether a
    permanent magnet or an electromagnet would be more suitable to remove
    the metal. Explain your answer.

    ....

    ....

    ....

> Electric charge

Exercise 5.3

IN THIS EXERCISE YOU WILL:

- recall key facts about the attractive and repulsive forces between electric charges
- check your understanding of electrostatic charging
- describe how an object gains an electrostatic charge by thinking about electrons and protons.

Focus

1 Copy and complete these sentences.

There are two types of electric charge, known as _____ and

_____.

An object can become charged if it is rubbed with a cloth. When the object is rubbed,

the force of _____ causes some of the negatively-charged particles,

called _____, to be transferred either from the cloth to the object or

from the object to the cloth.

If the object gains electrons it becomes _____ charged.

If the object loses electrons to the cloth, we say the object is _____

charged.

2 When charged objects are brought close together, they may attract or repel each other. State what will happen when the following pairs of objects are brought close together:

   a two positively-charged objects

   ....

   b two negatively-charged objects

   ....

KEY WORDS

electric field: a region where charged objects experience a force; the direction of the field at a point in the field is the direction of force on a positive charge at that point.

electron: a negatively-charged particle, smaller than an atom.

electrostatic charge: a property of an object that causes it to attract or repel other objects with charge.

negative charge: one of the two types of electric charge; the other is positive charge.

neutral: having no overall positive or negative electric charge.

positive charge: one of the two types of electric charge; the other is negative charge.

proton: a positively-charged particle found in the atomic nucleus.

c a positively-charged object and a negatively-charged object

....

d a positively-charged object and an uncharged object

....

e a negatively-charged object and an uncharged object.

....

> **TIP**
>
> Never talk about positive charge moving with static electricity. It is always (negative) electrons that move.

3 **a** State the name given to a material that allows electric charge to flow through it.

....

b Give an example of a material that allows charge to flow through it.

....

4 A learner rubs a plastic rod with a wool cloth. The rod gains a negative electrostatic charge.

Before the experiment, the rod had no electrostatic charge.

a State the one word that means 'having no electrostatic charge'. ....

b The learner wants to check that the rod has become charged. Describe a simple method they can use to show the rod has become charged.

....

....

....

Practice

5 **a** State what type of particles have been transferred to the rod in question **4**. Explain how you know.

....

....

b The cloth is left with a positive charge. State which type of particle the cloth has more of: protons or electrons. ....

6 A learner rubs a plastic rod with a wool cloth. Both the rod and the cloth become electrostatically charged.

a State the force that causes the two materials to become charged. ....

b The cloth has a positive electrostatic charge. State what type of charge the rod has. ....

c The cloth and rod are brought close to one another. State whether they will attract or repel each other. ....

d State why this happens.

....

7 Figure 5.6 shows one way in which the learner could observe the forces exerted by the electrostatically charged cloth and rod on each other.

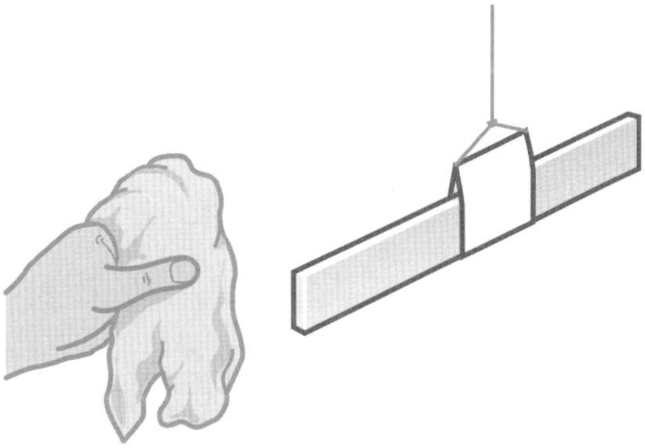

Figure 5.6: A diagram showing how the electrostatic forces between two charged objects might be observed.

Write a brief description of this experiment. Explain how it is done and describe what you would expect to observe.

....
....
....
....
....
....
....

Challenge

8 Explain why conductors allow electrostatic charge to flow through them, but other materials do not allow charge to flow through them.

....

....

....

....

....

....

9 A learner charges a plastic rod by rubbing. The rod becomes positively charged. She brings it close to another rod and the two rods attract. She concludes that the second rod must be negatively charged.

a State why this conclusion may be wrong.

....

....

b Describe what the learner would need to do to check her conclusion.

....

....

....

....

Exercise 5.4

Focus

1   It is easy to generate static electricity by rubbing two materials together. Both the materials must be electrical insulators and they must not be the same material.

Find some different plastic items such as pens, rulers and combs. Find some pieces of cloth made from cotton, polyester, wool and so on.

Rub one plastic item on one of the cloths. Test whether your item has become electrostatically charged by seeing if it will pick up scraps of paper. Use scraps of thin paper less than 5 mm in size.

Try different combinations of plastic items and cloths. Record your results in a table.

Briefly describe and explain your findings. In your answer:

- state whether one combination of materials is better than another at generating static electricity

- describe how you made this a fair test.

....

....

....

....

....

....

....

....

....

....

....

....

Practice

2   Use a comb on clean, dry hair that does not have any hair product in it
     (such as hair gel, conditioner, etc.). Pass the comb through the hair many times.

     Now bring the comb very close to (but *not* touching) a slow steady stream of
     water from a tap.

     a   Describe what you see happening.

     ....

     ....

     ....

     ....

     b   Explain your observations.

     ....

     ....

     ....

     ....

     ....

     ....

PEER ASSESSMENT

Discuss your explanation with your class. If you have missed any key points which come up in this discussion, use them to improve your explanation.

Challenge

3   Explain why we sometimes get a shock when we walk across a carpet and touch a
     door handle.

     ....

     ....

     ....

     ....

     ....

> Current, voltage and resistance

Exercise 5.5

KEY EQUATIONS

$I = \dfrac{Q}{t}$, where I = current in amps, Q = charge in coulombs and

t = time in seconds

$\text{resistance} = \dfrac{\text{potential difference}}{\text{current}}$

$R = \dfrac{V}{I}$

Focus

1 Complete the following sentences using the words from the list below.

> ammeter   conductors   amps   parallel   electrons   volts   cell
>
> potential difference   series   complete   charge   voltmeter

A current is a flow of electric _____, usually carried by

_____.

For current to flow, there must be a _____ circuit made up of

_____.

Current is measured in _____ using an _____

which is connected in _____.

The push supplied by a battery or _____ provides energy to make
the current flow.

KEY WORDS

amp, ampere (A): the SI unit of electric current.

battery: two or more electrical cells connected together in series; the word may also be used to mean a single cell.

cell: a device that provides an electromotive force (voltage) in a circuit by means of a chemical reaction.

conductor: a substance that allows an electric current to pass through it.

coulomb (C): the SI unit of electric charge.

current: a flow of electric charge; the charge passing a point in a circuit per second.

electromotive force (e.m.f): the voltage across a cell or power supply.

insulator: a substance that does not conduct electricity.

ohm (Ω): the SI unit of electrical resistance.

This push is called the _____ (or voltage) and is measured

in _____ using a _____ connected in

_____.

2 For an electric current to flow, it must have something to flow through. Complete Table 5.1 by putting a tick (✓) in the correct column to indicate whether each material is a conductor or an insulator.

Material	Conductor?	Insulator?
steel		
plastic		
glass		
copper		
silver		
wood		

Table 5.1

Practice

3 Describe an experiment, using an ammeter, which would allow you to prove that your answers to question **2** are correct. State what you would expect to see. Include a circuit diagram.

....

....

....

....

....

....

....

KEY WORDS

p.d. (potential difference): another name for the voltage between two points.

resistance: the ratio of the p.d. across a component to the current flowing through it.

resistor: a component in an electric circuit which limits or controls the flow of current.

volt (V): the SI unit of voltage (p.d. or e.m.f.).

voltage: the 'push' of a battery or power supply in a circuit.

TIP

Note the subtle difference between the definition of potential difference (p.d.) and the definition of electromotive force (e.m.f.): e.m.f is the p.d across a power supply.

Potential difference is the work done in moving +1 coulomb (C) *between two points in a circuit.* e.m.f. is the work done in moving +1 C *around the whole circuit.*

4   The circuit in Figure 5.7 has two meters. Their symbols are incomplete.

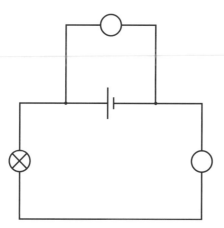

Figure 5.7: A simple circuit with two unknown meters.

a   Complete the symbol for the meter that measures the current. On Figure 5.7, label it with its name.

b   Complete the symbol for the meter that measures the voltage of the cell. On Figure 5.7, label it with its name.

c   State the name given to two or more cells connected together in a circuit.

....

Challenge

5   a   The equation $Q = It$ relates current, charge and time. Complete Table 5.2 to show the meaning of the symbols in this equation and give their units (name and symbol).

Symbol	Quantity	Unit (name and symbol)
Q		
I		
t		

Table 5.2

b   Write an equation linking the following units: coulomb, ampere and second.

....

6 **a** A current of 2.4 A flows in a circuit. State how much charge flows past a point in one second. ....

   b Calculate the charge that flows in 30 s.

   ....

7 An electric motor is supplied with current by a power supply. A charge of 720 C passes through the motor each minute. Calculate the current that is flowing.

   ....

8 A battery supplies a current of 1.25 A to a circuit. Calculate how long it will take for 75 C of charge to flow around the circuit.

   ....

Exercise 5.6

IN THIS EXERCISE YOU WILL:

- show how the resistance of a component tells us how easy (or difficult) it is to make current flow through that component

- practise calculations using the equation $R = \dfrac{V}{I}$.

Focus

1 We say that an ohm (Ω) is a volt (V) per ampere (A). So, if a resistor has a resistance of 10 Ω, it takes 10 V to make a current of 1 A flow through it.

   a Calculate the voltage needed to make a current of 2 A flow through the same 10 Ω resistor.

   ....

   b Calculate the voltage needed to make a current of 1 A flow through a 20 Ω resistor.

   ....

Practice

2   The current in a circuit changes as the resistance in the circuit changes. Complete
    Table 5.3 to show whether each change will cause the current to increase or
    to decrease.

Change	Current – increase or decrease?
more resistance in the circuit	
less resistance in the circuit	
increase the voltage	

Table 5.3

3   Use the equation $R = \dfrac{V}{I}$ to calculate the resistance of a lamp if a p.d. of 36 V
    makes a current of 4.5 A flow through it.

    ....

4   Rearrange the equation given in question **3** to make:

    a V the subject of the equation ....

    b I the subject of the equation. ....

Challenge

5   Calculate the missing values in Table 5.4. Remember to check the units and
    convert them if necessary.

Voltage	Current	Resistance
12 V	0.5 A	
230 V	4 A	
	2 A	30 Ω
	100 mA	45 Ω
230 V		20 Ω
12 V		10 kΩ

Table 5.4

6 A learner measured the resistance of a resistor. To do this, she set up a circuit in which the resistor was connected to a variable power supply, a voltmeter and an ammeter.

a In the space below, draw a circuit diagram to show these components connected together correctly so that the learner could measure the current in the resistor and the p.d. across it.

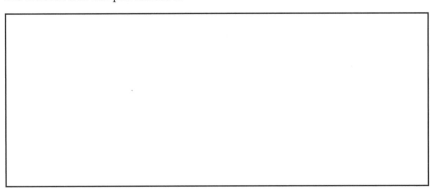

b Table 5.5 shows the learner's results. Complete the third column. The first one has been done for you.

p.d. V/V	Current I/A	Resistance R/Ω
2.0	0.37	5.4
4.1	0.75	
5.9	1.20	
7.9	1.60	

Table 5.5

c Calculate an average value for the resistance R of the resistor.

....

Exercise 5.7

IN THIS EXERCISE YOU WILL:

- discuss how changing the length or diameter of a wire alters its resistance.

Focus

1 How does doubling the length of a wire change its resistance?

....

Practice

2 How does doubling the diameter of a wire affect its resistance?

....

Challenge

3 A wire has a resistance of 5 Ω. Calculate the resistance of a wire of the same material that is three times as long and has twice the diameter.

....

〉 Electrical energy and electrical power

Exercise 5.8

IN THIS EXERCISE YOU WILL:

- recall that power is the rate at which energy is transferred

- practise your understanding of power in electrical circuits.

KEY EQUATIONS

power = current × p.d.

$$P = I \times V$$

energy transformed = current × voltage × time

$$E = I \times V \times t$$

energy (kWh) = power of appliance (kW) × time used (hours)

cost of using an electrical appliance = power of appliance (kW) × time used (hours) × cost per unit

KEY WORDS

power: the rate at which work is done or energy is transferred.

watt (W): the SI unit of power; 1 W = 1 J/s.

Focus

1 **a** Write down an equation linking power, energy transformed and time. Include the symbols and units for all the quantities involved.

....

b Write down an equation linking power, current and voltage. Include the symbols and units for all the quantities involved.

....

Practice

2 An electric motor is connected to a 12 V direct current (d.c.) supply. A current of 0.25 A flows through the motor.

Calculate the power of the motor.

....

....

3 An electrical appliance has a label that indicates its power. The label includes the following data:

110 V   500 W   50 Hz

a State the power rating of the appliance. ....

b State how much energy it transfers each second. ....

c Calculate the current that will flow when the appliance is in normal use.

....

....

> **TIP**
>
> Compare a 40 watt (W) lamp and a 100 W lamp, both of which are at normal brightness with 230 V across them. Which has the higher resistance?
>
> Power is given by $P = I \times V$ but the p.d. across both lamps is the same. Therefore, it is an increase in current that causes the increase in power (from 40 W to 100 W).
>
> To have a larger current with the same potential difference, the 100 W lamp must have a lower resistance (from $V = I \times R$, so $I = \dfrac{V}{R}$).
>
> The 40 W lamp has the higher resistance.

> **TIP**
>
> Electricity calculations often involve conversions between units, such as kW to W or minutes to seconds. Watch out for these.

4   A learner investigated the cost of the electrical energy she uses in her room.
    She recorded the power of each device she used and the time she used it for.
    She checked the cost of electricity and found it was 8 rupees per kWh.
    The mains voltage is 230 V.

Device	Power	Time used for	Energy used/kWh	Cost/rupees
Lamp	60 W	3 hours		
Heater	1.5 kW	1 hour		
Computer	200 W	4 hours		
Hairdryer	2 kW	20 minutes		

Table 5.6

a   Calculate the energy used by each device (remember to convert units
    when needed). Record your answers in Table 5.6.

b   Calculate the cost of using each device for the time shown. Record your
    answers in Table 5.6.

c   The girl wants to reduce the amount of energy she uses to help reduce
    the bill. What advice would you give her?

    ....

    ....

    ....

Challenge

5   A lamp has a resistance of 600 Ω.

a   Calculate the current that flows through the lamp when it is connected to a
    240 V mains supply.

    ....

    ....

b   Calculate the power of the lamp.

    ....

    ....

6 Complete Table 5.7. Assume the cost per kWh is 20 pence.

Potential difference/V	Current/A	Power/W	Time used for/min	Cost of use for this time/pence
200		600		3.6
	2.72	600	90	
120	4			16
200 000		300 000	10	1000
220		100	240	

Table 5.7

PEER ASSESSMENT

Draw a mind map of the chapter, then compare your mind map to those of others. Make sure you include all the equations you have met, including the symbols and units for the quantities. Give and receive feedback on the mind maps.

You can also try writing some questions which require calculations using the equations in this chapter. Swap questions with a partner and answer each other's questions. Mark your partner's work and give them feedback. Consider:

- Have they written down the correct equation?

- Have they rearranged the equation if needed?

- Have they substituted the correct values into the equation?

- Is their calculation correct?

- Have they given a unit for their answer?

> Chapter 6

Electrical circuits

> Describing circuits

Exercise 6.1

IN THIS EXERCISE YOU WILL:

- practise applying your understanding of circuit components, their symbols and functions
- practise drawing series and parallel circuit diagrams
- describe the difference between series and parallel circuits.

KEY WORDS

ammeter: a meter for measuring electric current.

cell: a device that provides an electromotive force (voltage) in a circuit by means of a chemical reaction.

parallel circuit: a circuit in which there is more than one path which the current can take.

resistor: a component in an electric circuit which limits or controls the flow of current.

series circuit: a circuit in which there is only one path the current can take around the circuit.

variable resistor: a resistor whose resistance can be changed, for example by turning a knob.

voltmeter: a meter for measuring voltage or potential difference.

Focus

1   On Table 6.1, draw the symbol for each of these components.

lamp	resistor	variable resistor
ammeter	voltmeter	switch
cell		

Table 6.1

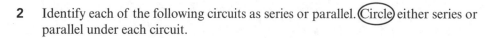

2   Identify each of the following circuits as series or parallel. Circle either series or parallel under each circuit.

a

series   parallel

b

series   parallel

c

series   parallel

d

series   parallel

Practice

3   Complete Table 6.2 by identifying each component described in the first column.

Description	Component
gives out heat and light	
provides the 'push' to make a current flow	
'blows' when the current is too high	
makes and breaks a circuit	
adjusted to change the resistance in a circuit	

Table 6.2

4 a In the space below, draw a circuit diagram showing a cell lighting two lamps which are connected in series.

b In the space below, draw a circuit diagram showing a cell lighting two lamps which are connected in parallel.

5 Each of the circuits in Figure 6.1 and Figure 6.2 has a mistake which means the circuit will not work as intended. For each circuit, identify and describe the mistake. Then draw the circuit with the mistake corrected.

a A circuit to measure the voltage across two lamps which are connected in series.

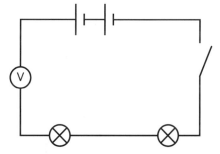

Figure 6.1: A series circuit with a mistake in it.

Mistake: ....

Corrected circuit:

b   A circuit to light two lamps connected in series.

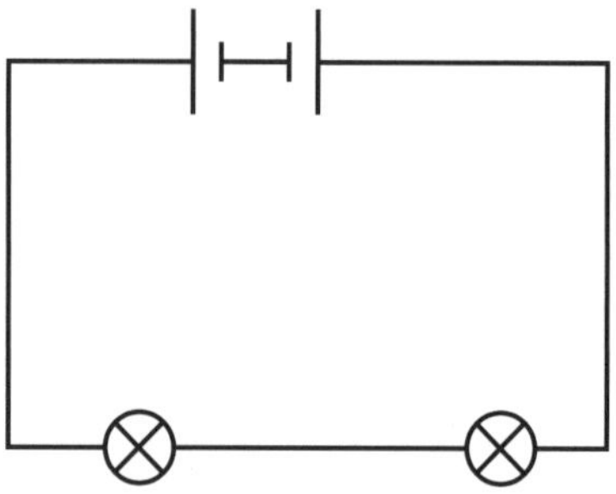

Figure 6.2: A series circuit with a mistake in it.

Mistake: ....
Corrected circuit:

6 The two lamps in Figure 6.3 are identical.

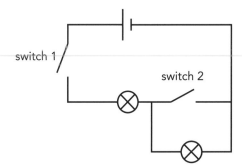

Figure 6.3: A circuit with two lamps controlled by two switches.

Describe and explain what happens to the lamps when:

a switch 1 is closed and switch 2 is open

....

....

b switch 1 and switch 2 are both open

....

....

c switch 1 and switch 2 are both closed.

....

....

Challenge

7 In the space below, draw a circuit diagram with a cell, three lamps and two switches. Two lamps should be controlled by the same switch. The third lamp should be controlled by its own switch.

8   In the space below, draw a circuit diagram in which a cell is used to light a lamp. Include a switch to turn the lamp on and off. Also include the correct components to measure the current through the lamp and the voltage across it.

9   A hairdryer contains a heater and a fan.

- When hot air is required, the heater and fan are both switched on. The heater becomes hot. The fan blows cold air over the heater, so hot air is blown out of the hairdryer.

- The hairdryer can also be operated to give cold air. For this, only the fan is switched on.

- For safety reasons, it must not be possible to turn on the heater without the fan. This could cause the hairdryer to overheat.

a   In the space below, draw a circuit diagram for the hairdryer. The fan is operated by a motor, so use the motor symbol to show the fan. The symbols are shown in Figure 6.4.

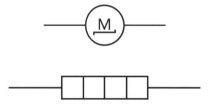

Figure 6.4: Circuit symbols for a motor and a heating coil.

b Explain what should be done to:

i make the hairdryer blow hot air

....

....

ii make the hairdryer blow cold air.

....

....

PEER ASSESSMENT

Look back at the circuits you have drawn. Use this table to show your progress. Draw a smiley face if you did well and draw a face with a straight line if you are nearly there. If you are not sure, leave the box blank.

Task	How did I do?
I drew all the symbols correctly.	
I connected the symbols correctly with straight lines.	
I can identify whether a circuit is series or parallel.	
I can draw a series circuit.	
I can draw a parallel circuit.	

Table 6.3

Discuss your table with others in your class. If they have left any boxes blank, try to explain to them how they can improve.

Exercise 6.2

IN THIS EXERCISE YOU WILL:

- practise applying your understanding of circuit components, their symbols and functions

- practise drawing series and parallel circuit diagrams

- describe the difference between series and parallel circuits.

Focus

1 Figure 6.5 shows a series circuit with ammeters measuring the current at different points in the circuit.

    a Ammeter A_1 gives a reading of 0.5 A. State the reading on:

       i Ammeter A_2

....

      ii Ammeter A_3.

....

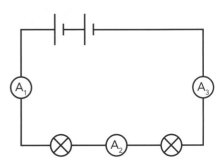

Figure 6.5: A series circuit.

    b The lamp between ammeters 1 and 2 is unscrewed. State what will happen to the other lamp.

....

Practice

2 Figure 6.6 shows a circuit with two lamps connected in parallel. The circuit contains ammeters to measure the current at different points in the circuit.

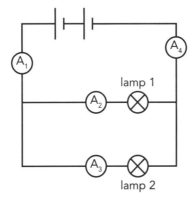

Figure 6.6: A parallel circuit.

a   Ammeter A$_1$ gives a reading of 1 A. (Circle) the correct value for each of the
     other three ammeters.

    i   A$_2$ reads: 1 A / less than 1 A / more than 1 A

    ii   A$_3$ reads: 1 A / less than 1 A / more than 1 A

    iii A$_4$ reads: 1 A / less than 1 A / more than 1 A

b   Lamp 1 is unscrewed. State what will happen to lamp 2.

    ....

c   The lights in a house are connected in parallel rather than in series.
     Explain why it is better to connect the lights in parallel.

    ....

    ....

Challenge

3   a   Two resistors are connected in series to a 12 V power supply. The voltage
         across one of the resistors is 10 V. What is the voltage across the
         second resistor?

      ....

      ....

   b   The same two resistors are now connected in parallel with the 12 V supply.
         What are the voltages across the two resistors in parallel?

      ....

      ....

> Resistors

Exercise 6.3

IN THIS EXERCISE YOU WILL:	KEY EQUATION

IN THIS EXERCISE YOU WILL:

- practise applying your knowledge and understanding of how current flows in a circuit with more than one resistor

- calculate the combined resistance of resistors in series

- describe the effect of connecting resistors in parallel.

KEY EQUATION

resistors in series:
$R = R_1 + R_2 + R_3$

Focus

1   Figure 6.7 shows a series circuit with a lamp, an ammeter and a resistor.

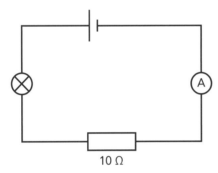

10 Ω

Figure 6.7: A series circuit with a cell, a lamp, a labelled resistor and an ammeter.

A second 10 Ω resistor is added in series with the resistor shown in Figure 6.7.

a   In the space below, draw the new circuit.

b State what will happen to:

    i the brightness of the lamp (increases / decreases / stays the same)

    ....

    ii the current measured by the ammeter (increases / decreases / stays the

    same) ....

    iii the total resistance in the circuit (increases / decreases / stays the same).

    ....

The extra resistor is now moved so it is connected in parallel with the first resistor.

c In the space below, draw the new circuit.

d State what will happen to:

    i the brightness of the lamp (increases / decreases / stays the same)

    ....

    ii the current measured by the ammeter (increases / decreases / stays the

    same) ....

    iii the total resistance in the circuit (increases / decreases / stays the same).

    ....

2 Calculate the combined resistance of three $30\,\Omega$ resistors connected in series.

....

Practice

3   Look at the circuit shown in Figure 6.8.

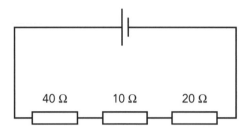

Figure 6.8: A circuit with three labelled resistors and a cell.

a   State whether the three resistors are connected in series or in parallel.

....

b   Calculate the combined resistance of the three resistors in the circuit.

....

c   What can you state about the current in each of the three resistors?

....

4   Look at the circuit shown in Figure 6.9.

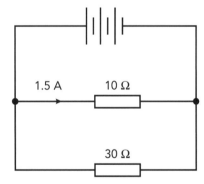

Figure 6.9: A circuit with a battery and two labelled resistors.

a   State whether the two resistors are connected in series or in parallel.

....

b   One of the following statements is true. Tick (✓) the correct one.

A   The combined resistance of the two resistors must be less than 10 Ω.   ☐

B   The combined resistance of the two resistors must be more than 40 Ω.   ☐

Challenge

5   Figure 6.9 shows that the current in the 10 Ω resistor is 1.5 A. State what you know about:

a   the current leaving the battery

   ....

b   the current in the 30 Ω resistor.

   ....

〉 Circuit calculations

Exercise 6.4

IN THIS EXERCISE YOU WILL:

*   practise applying your knowledge and understanding of series and parallel circuits.

Focus

1   Calculate the combined resistance of two 120 Ω resistors connected:

a   in series

   ....

b   in parallel.

   ....

2   The three lamps in Figure 6.10 are all identical. The reading on Ammeter 1 is 1.5 A.

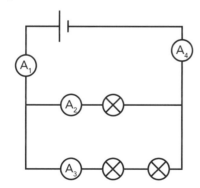

Figure 6.10: A parallel circuit with three lamps.

Determine the reading on each of these ammeters.

a A$_2$ ....

b A$_3$ ....

c A$_4$ ....

Practice

3   Figure 6.11 shows three resistors connected to a battery.

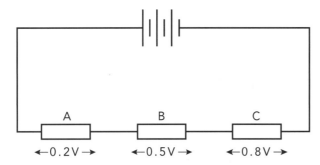

Figure 6.11: A circuit with a battery and three resistors, A, B and C.

a   By comparing the potential differences across the resistors, determine which

resistor has the greatest resistance. ....

b   A current of 0.15 A flows through resistor A. Calculate the resistance of
resistor C.

....

....

c   Calculate the p.d. of the battery.

....

....

4   In Figure 6.12, resistors A and B are connected in parallel with a 12 V cell.
The current flowing from the battery and the current through resistor A are
marked on the diagram.

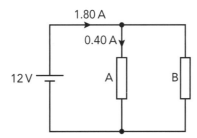

Figure 6.12: A circuit with a cell and two resistors in parallel.

a   Calculate the resistance of resistor A.

....

b   Explain the benefit of wiring devices in parallel.

....

....

c   Calculate the current through resistor B. Explain your answer.

....

....

d   Calculate the resistance of resistor B.

....

Challenge

5   Calculate the combined (effective) resistance of resistors A and B in Figure 6.12.

....

....

....

6   Calculate the total resistance of the combination of resistors shown in Figure 6.13.

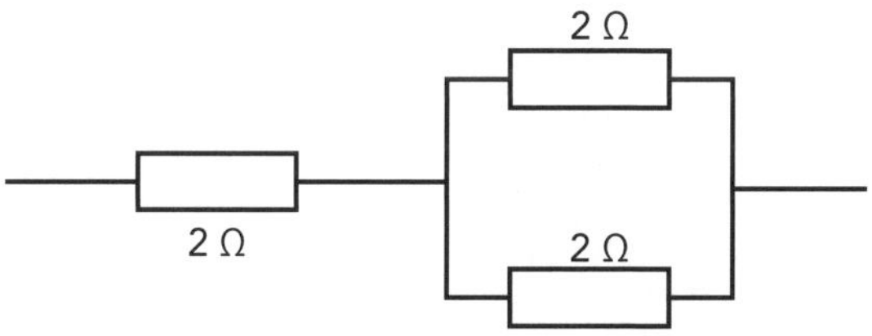

Figure 6.13: A combination of three resistors.

....

....

....

> Electrical safety

Exercise 6.5

IN THIS EXERCISE YOU WILL:

- describe how we use mains electricity safely

- select the fuse needed for an appliance.

Focus

1   Many countries do not allow light switches or power sockets to be fitted in bathrooms. Explain why this is the case.

....

Practice

2   Figure 6.14 shows a situation which causes an electrical hazard. Describe the safety issue shown in the image.

Figure 6.14: A domestic wall socket in use.

....

....

....

3   **a**   Explain the operation of a fuse.

....

....

b   Explain why a fuse is a safety device.

....

....

Challenge

4   An electric heater has a current of 8.0 A in normal use. The fuse fitted in the plug has 'blown' and needs to be replaced. The following three fuses are available:

5 A, 10 A and 30 A.

For each possible value, state and explain whether it would be suitable or unsuitable.

a   5 A: ....

....

....

b   10 A: ....

....

....

c   30 A: ....

....

....

5   When a fuse 'blows', it must be replaced. Name the alternative device that can be used in a circuit, that can be reset each time it breaks the circuit.

....

Chapter 7

Electromagnetic effects

> Magnetic effect of current

Exercise 7.1

IN THIS EXERCISE YOU WILL:
• practise applying your understanding of the magnetic effect of an electric current
• describe how the strength and polarity of magnetic fields can be changed.

KEY WORD

right-hand grip rule: the rule used to determine the direction of the magnetic field around a wire carrying an electric current.

Focus

1 A magnetic field forms around a wire carrying current. The direction of the magnetic field lines is given by the 'right-hand grip rule'. You imagine gripping the wire with your right hand.

Complete the following sentences:

a The direction of your thumb tells you the direction of ....

b The direction in which your fingers curl round the wire tells you the direction

of ....

Practice

2 Describe an experiment to establish the shape of the magnetic field around a long straight wire.

....

....

....

....

....

....

....

....

....

3   In the space below, sketch the magnetic field around a solenoid that is carrying
    a current.
    Label the direction of the current flow and the direction of the field lines.

Challenge

4   **a**   Describe the effect on the magnetic field around a solenoid of increasing the
            current flowing through the solenoid.

    ....

    ....

    b   State how the polarity of the solenoid could be reversed.

    ....

    ....

> Force on a current-carrying conductor

Exercise 7.2

IN THIS EXERCISE YOU WILL:

- practise applying your understanding of the force on a current-carrying conductor.

Focus

1 State how the direction of the force on a current-carrying conductor could be reversed.

....

....

....

Practice

2 Fleming's left-hand rule gives the direction of the force on a current-carrying conductor in a magnetic field.

a Label the thumb and first two fingers of the left hand in Figure 7.1 to show what they represent.

Figure 7.1: Fleming's left-hand rule.

b Use Fleming's left-hand rule to find the direction of the force on the wire in Figure 7.2. State whether the force will push the wire into the page or out of the page.

Figure 7.2: A current-carrying wire between two magnets.

Challenge

3 The apparatus shown in Figure 7.3 is used to demonstrate the force on a current-carrying conductor in a magnetic field.

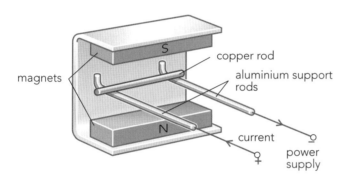

Figure 7.3: Equipment used to demonstrate the force on a current-carrying conductor at right angles to a magnetic field.

a On Figure 7.3, draw a line on the diagram to show the direction of the magnetic field.

b In this arrangement, the force on the copper rod will make it roll towards the power supply.

Describe the effect of reversing the direction of the current.

....

....

....

....

c   State *two* ways in which the force on the copper rod could be increased.

....

....

....

....

> The d.c. motor

Exercise 7.3

IN THIS EXERCISE YOU WILL:

- explain how an electric motor is constructed
- describe ways of changing the speed and direction of rotation of a motor.

KEY WORDS

commutator: a device used to allow current to flow to and from the coil of a d.c. motor or generator.

electromagnet: a coil of wire that becomes a magnet when a current flows in it.

Focus

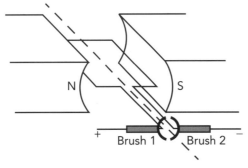

Figure 7.4: An electric motor.

1   a   An electric motor (Figure 7.4) can be made using a coil of wire that rotates in a magnetic field.

Name the part of the motor that acts as an electromagnet.

....

b   Electric current enters and leaves the coil via two brushes.

Name the part of the motor that the brushes press against, to transfer the

current to the coil. ....

2   State *three* ways in which the turning effect of a d.c. motor can be increased.

....

....

....

....

Practice

3   Describe the effect on a motor if the directions of both the magnetic field and the
current are reversed, and the current is increased.

....

....

....

Challenge

4   a   State what would be observed if alternating current was passed through the
coil of a d.c. motor.

....

b   A learner built a motor to run on a d.c. supply. The learner forgot to include a
commutator. State what the learner will observe when the motor is switched on.

....

> Electromagnetic induction

Exercise 7.4

IN THIS EXERCISE YOU WILL:

- check your understanding of electromagnetic induction.

KEY WORD

electromagnetic induction: the process by which a potential difference is induced across a conductor when the magnetic field around it changes.

Focus

1 Complete Table 7.1 to show whether a current will be induced (made to flow) in each case. Assume that the wire is always part of a complete circuit. Write 'Yes' or 'No' in the second column.

Case	Is a current induced?
A wire is moved through the field of a magnet.	
A magnet is held close to a wire.	
A magnet is moved into a coil of wire.	
A magnet is moved out of a coil of wire.	
A magnet rests in a coil of wire.	

Table 7.1

Practice

2 State *four* ways in which the induced e.m.f. across a coil of wire could be increased.

....

....

....

3 The direction of rotation is reversed. State how this affects the induced e.m.f.

....

Challenge

4   State the *one* factor that links all of your answers to question **2**.
Explain your answer.

....

....

....

....

> The a.c. generator

Exercise 7.5

IN THIS EXERCISE YOU WILL:

- describe how an a.c. generator works

- show how the change in e.m.f. produced over time is related to the position of an a.c. generator coil.

TIP

When studying electromagnetic effects, you come across three terms that seem to describe the same thing: voltage, potential difference and electromotive force. This can be confusing. Remember:

- potential difference is the work done in moving one coulomb of charge between two points in a circuit

- electromotive force is the work done in moving one coulomb of charge around the entire circuit

- voltage is a more general term and can refer to either potential difference or electromotive force.

KEY WORDS

a.c. generator: a device, such as a dynamo, used to generate alternating current (a.c.).

slip rings: a component used to allow current to flow to and from the coil of an a.c. motor or generator.

Focus

1   Alternating current is generated using an a.c. generator. This is similar to an electric motor, working in reverse. Write the missing word to complete these sentences.

An a.c. generator does not have a commutator. Instead, current enters and leaves

the spinning coil through brushes that press on the _____

Practice

2   Figure 7.5 shows how an alternating current varies with time. On the figure, mark one cycle of the alternating current.

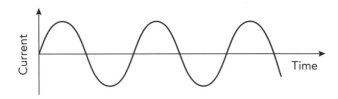

Figure 7.5: The variation of alternating current with time.

Challenge

3   On Figure 7.6, which is a larger version of Figure 7.5, draw the position of the coil when the current is:

a   a maximum positive value

b   zero

c   a maximum negative value.

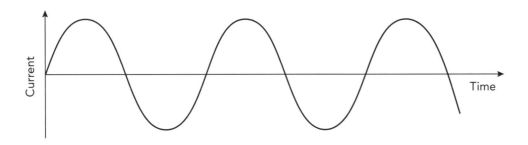

Figure 7.6: The variation of alternating current with time.

> The transformer

Exercise 7.6

KEY EQUATIONS

$$\frac{\text{voltage across primary coil}}{\text{voltage across secondary coil}} = \frac{\text{number of turns on primary coil}}{\text{number of turns on secondary coil}}$$

$$\frac{V_p}{V_s} = \frac{N_p}{N_s}$$

power into primary coil = power out of secondary coil

$$I_p \times V_p = I_s \times V_s$$

power = current^2 × resistance

$$P = I^2 R$$

Focus

1 a Figure 7.7 shows a step-up transformer.

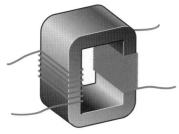

Figure 7.7: A step-up transformer.

State which coil has more turns in a step-up transformer.

....

b On Figure 7.7, label the primary coil, the secondary coil and the iron core.

Practice

2   In the circuit diagram in Figure 7.8, a transformer is being used to change the mains voltage to a lower value so that it will light a 12 V lamp.

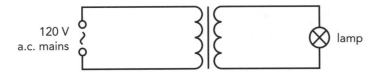

Figure 7.8: A mains transformer used to power a 12 V lamp.

a   State whether this is a step-up or step-down transformer.

....

b   The primary coil has 1000 turns. Calculate the number of turns on the secondary coil.

....

....

....

3   At a small power station, the generator produces alternating current at a voltage of 10 kV. This must be reduced to 415 V for use in a factory.

a   The transformer used for this purpose has 2000 turns on the primary coil. Calculate the number of turns on the secondary coil.

....

....

....

b   The current flowing from the generator is 4.5 A. Calculate the power that is being generated.

....

....

....

c   Calculate the current flowing in the power lines in the factory. Assume that all of the electrical power generated is transmitted to the factory.

....

....

....

Challenge

4   An overhead power line has a resistance of $2.5\,\Omega$. By considering the power losses, find the increase in efficiency when transmitting $100\,MW$ of electrical energy along this cable at:

a $20\,000\,V$

....

....

....

b $400\,000\,V$.

....

....

....

PEER ASSESSMENT

Write a set of flash cards or draw a mind map to summarise this chapter. Swap your work with others in your class and offer feedback to each other.

What was the thing you liked best about the other person's work? Was there anything that you felt needed further development?

Chapter 8

Nuclear physics

> The nuclear atom

Exercise 8.1

KEY EQUATION

proton number + neutron number = nucleon number

Focus

1 Name the two types of particle that make up the nucleus of a sodium atom.

....

....

2 Figure 8.1 shows a simple model of an atom.

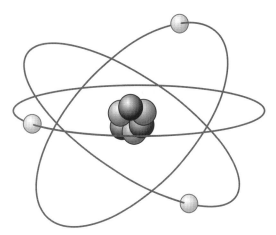

Figure 8.1: A simple model of an atom.

a   On Figure 8.1, label the nucleus and an electron.

b   State which part of the atom contains most of its mass.

....

c   State which part of the atom contains all of its positive charge.

....

Practice

3   The nucleus of a particular atom of oxygen (O) is made up of eight protons and eight neutrons. In the space below, write the symbol for this nucleus in the form: $_Z^A X$.

4   Complete Table 8.1 to identify the number of protons and the number of neutrons for each nucleus.

Nucleus	Number of protons	Number of neutrons
$_4^9 Be$		
$_9^{19} F$		
$_{20}^{40} Ca$		
$_{80}^{201} Hg$		

Table 8.1

Challenge

5   A particular atom of carbon (C) is represented like this: $_6^{13} C$.

a   State the value of the proton number Z for this atom.

....

b   State the value of the nucleon number A for this atom.

....

c   Calculate the value of the neutron number N for this atom.

....

6   Complete Table 8.2 by identifying the subatomic particles described.

Description	Proton, neutron or electron?
These particles make up the nucleus. [There are two answers.]	
These particles orbit the nucleus.	
These particles have very little mass.	
These particles have no electric charge.	
The charge on these particles is equal and opposite to the charge on an electron.	

Table 8.2

Exercise 8.2

IN THIS EXERCISE YOU WILL:

- check your recall and understanding of isotopes and use your knowledge to identify some elements in the Periodic Table.

Focus

1   **a**   State what is the same for two isotopes of an element.

   ....

   b   State what is different for two isotopes of an element.

   ....

2   Two of the nuclei listed below are isotopes. Circle the isotopes.

$^{14}_{7}\text{N}$ $^{40}_{19}\text{K}$ $^{40}_{18}\text{Ar}$ $^{15}_{7}\text{N}$ $^{20}_{10}\text{Ne}$

Practice

3   Figure 8.2 represents an atom of an isotope of boron (B).

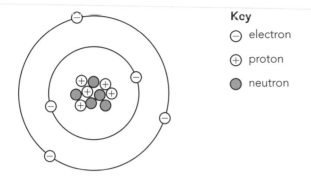

Key
⊖ electron
⊕ proton
● neutron

Figure 8.2: The structure of an atom of an isotope of boron.

Write down the symbol for this nuclide in the form: $^A_Z X$

....

Challenge

4   Table 8.3 shows some values of Z, N and A for six different nuclides.
Complete the table as follows:

- Fill in the missing values of Z, N and A in the second, third and fourth columns.
- Use the Periodic Table to identify the elements. Write your answers in the fifth column.
- In the last column, write the symbol for each nuclide in the form $^A_Z X$.

Nuclide	Proton number, Z	Neutron number, N	Nucleon number, A	Name of element	Nuclide symbol $^A_Z X$
Nu-1	4	5			
Nu-2	5	7			
Nu-3		4	8		
Nu-4	6		11		
Nu-5		6	11		

Table 8.3

> Radioactivity

Exercise 8.3

IN THIS EXERCISE YOU WILL:

- describe the three types of ionising nuclear radiation.

TIP

The properties and the natures of the three types of radiation are very clearly connected. Seeing that connection will help you to remember the key information.

An alpha particle is *very* large and heavy. It has about 8000 times the mass of a beta particle. Because it is large, it has a lot of collisions with the material it is passing through. As a result, it is easily stopped and has a short range in air. Because it has a lot of mass, it does a lot of damage when it collides with atoms – it is very ionising.

Gamma is electromagnetic radiation. It has no intrinsic mass and no charge, so it does not interact with matter as much as alpha or beta. This means it has a *very* large range in air and is difficult to stop. It also means that it is not very ionising.

Focus

1   Name the *three* types of ionising radiation and give the symbol used to represent each type.

   ....

   ....

   ....

2   **a**   Name a detector which can be used to measure the amount of ionising nuclear radiation emitted by a source.

   ....

   b   What units are used in the measurement of ionising nuclear radiation?

   ....

KEY WORDS

alpha decay: the decay of a radioactive nucleus by emission of an alpha particle; the general equation for this decay is $^{A}_{Z}X = ^{A-4}_{Z-2}Y + ^{4}_{2}\alpha$.

alpha particle (α-particle): a particle of two protons and two neutrons emitted by an atomic nucleus during radioactive decay.

background radiation: the nuclear radiation from the environment to which we are exposed all the time, due to the disintegration of unstable nuclei.

beta decay: the decay of a radioactive nucleus by emission of a beta particle.

beta particle (β-particle): an electron emitted by a nucleus during radioactive decay.

count rate: the number of nuclear disintegrations per second; measured in counts/min or counts/s.

3   List:

   a   *two* natural sources of background radiation

   •   ....

   •   ....

   b   *two* man-made sources of background radiation.

   •   ....

   •   ....

4   Figure 8.3 shows how the three types of radiation from radioactive substances are absorbed by different materials.

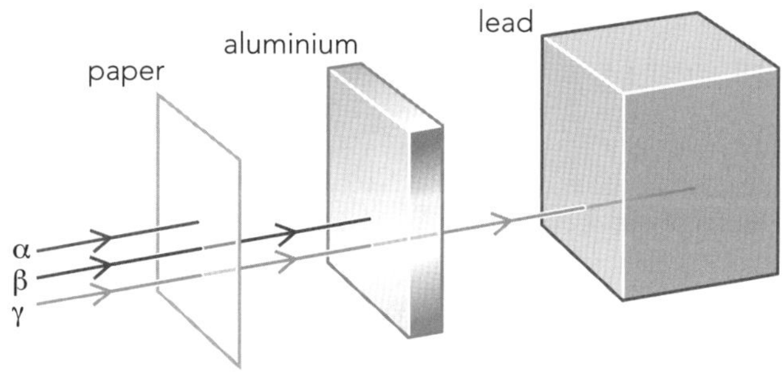

Figure 8.3: A comparison of how the three types of radiation are absorbed by different materials.

   a   Figure 8.3 uses symbols. Write the full names of those symbols.

   i α...

   ii β...

   iii γ...

   b   State which type of radiation is the most penetrating.

   ....

   c   State which type of radiation can be stopped by a few centimetres of air or by a thin sheet of paper.

   ....

   d   State which types of radiation are absorbed by a thick sheet of lead.

   ....

KEY WORDS

gamma ray (γ-ray): electromagnetic radiation emitted by an atomic nucleus during radioactive decay.

half-life: the average time taken for half the atoms in a sample of a radioactive material to decay.

ionising radiation: radiation, for example from radioactive substances, that causes ionisation.

penetration: how far radiation can travel into different materials.

radiation: energy spreading out from a source carried by particles or waves.

radioactive decay: the disintegration of the nucleus of a radioactive substance, when its nuclei emit radiation.

radioactive substance: a substance that decays by emitting radiation from its atomic nuclei.

random process: a process that happens at a random rate rather than at a steady rate; in radioactive decay, it is impossible to predict which atom will decay next, or when a given atom will decay.

e State which type of ionising radiation travels at the speed of light.

....

f State which type of ionising radiation has a negative charge.

....

g State which type of ionising radiation is a form of electromagnetic radiation.

....

Practice

5 The radiation from radioactive substances is called 'ionising radiation'.
This is because it can damage atoms, causing them to become ions.

a State which type of ionising radiation has no mass.

....

b State which type of ionising radiation has a positive charge.

....

c State which type of ionising radiation is an electron.

....

d State which type of ionising radiation is the same as a helium nucleus.

....

Challenge

6 Figure 8.4 shows the count rate measured after each of the barriers shown.
The source is on the left.

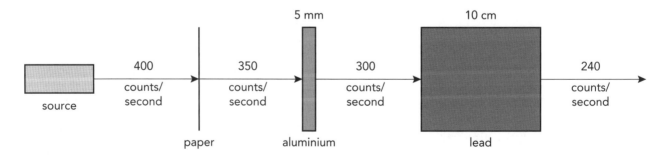

Figure 8.4: A diagram showing changing count rates through various materials.

a Calculate how many alpha particles were emitted per second.

....

b Calculate how many beta particles were emitted per second.

....

c State the background radiation count.

....

Exercise 8.4

IN THIS EXERCISE YOU WILL:

- explain nuclear decay
- practise writing and interpreting nuclide equations.

Focus

1 State what radioactive decay is.

....

2 Two types of particle can be emitted during radioactive decay, alpha and beta. Table 8.4 shows the symbols used for these particles when we write decay equations.

In the last column of the table, state the composition of each particle in terms of the subatomic particles: protons, neutrons and electrons.

Particle	Symbol	Composition
alpha, α	^4_2He	
beta, β	$^0_{-1}\text{e}$	

Table 8.4

Practice

3 Describe what is meant by radioactive decay. In your description, include:

- the types of decay
- their effect on the parent nucleus
- nuclear equations, as appropriate.

....

....

....

....

....

4 **a** State which type of radioactive emission does not change the number of protons or neutrons in the nucleus.

....

b State what happens to the proton number when an alpha particle is emitted.

....

c State what happens to the proton number when a beta particle is emitted.

....

5 The equation shows how an isotope of radium decays to become an isotope of radon.

$$^{223}_{88}\text{Ra} \rightarrow ^{219}_{86}\text{Rn} + ^{4}_{2}\text{He} + \text{energy}$$

a State the chemical symbol for radium. ....

b State the chemical symbol for radon. ....

c State the type of particle that is emitted. ....

We can check that the equation is balanced by counting the number of nucleons before and after the decay, and the number of protons before and after.

For the nucleons, we have $223 = 219 + 4$

d Show that the number of protons is the same before and after the decay.

....

6   The equation shows how an isotope of carbon decays to become an isotope
    of nitrogen.

$$^{15}_{6}\text{C} \rightarrow {}^{15}_{7}\text{N} + {}^{0}_{-1}\text{e} + \text{energy}$$

Show that this equation is balanced.

....

7   Complete the following decay equation, which shows how an isotope of polonium
    decays to become an isotope of lead:

$$^{211}_{84}\text{Po} \rightarrow {}^{207}_{82}\text{Pb} + \text{...}$$

Challenge

8   A student reads that a beta particle is a high-speed electron emitted from the
    nucleus. He says that this must be wrong because the nucleus does not contain
    any electrons.

    Explain to the student how what he has read can be true.

    ....

    ....

    ....

9   An isotope of protactinium (symbol Pa) has 91 protons and 140 neutrons in
    its nucleus.

    a   Write the symbol for this nuclide. ....

    The nuclide decays by alpha decay to become an isotope of actinium
    (symbol Ac).

    b   Write a complete decay equation for this decay.

        ....

10 $^{238}_{92}\text{U}$ decays by alpha decay, then beta decay, then beta decay.

    a   Deduce the nucleon number and the proton number of the nucleus produced
        after the third decay.

        ....

        ....

    b   State what element the nucleus has become.

        ....

Exercise 8.5

IN THIS EXERCISE YOU WILL:

* check your understanding of half-life.

Focus

1 A student writes:

The half-life of carbon-14 is 5730 years. After 11460 years, all the carbon-14 will have decayed. **Explain why the student's statement is wrong.**

....

....

....

2 A sample of a radioactive substance contains 2400 undecayed atoms.

a Calculate the number of atoms that will remain after three half-lives.

....

....

....

b Calculate the number of atoms that will decay during three half-lives.

....

....

....

c Explain why these calculations are not likely to match actual measurements.

....

....

3 A sample of a radioactive substance contains 1000 undecayed atoms. Its half-life is 4.5 years. Calculate the number of unstable atoms that will remain undecayed after 9 years.

....

4   The graph in Figure 8.5 shows the amount of the radioactive isotope iodine-131 at different times. Use the graph to determine the half-life of the isotope. Show your working on the graph.

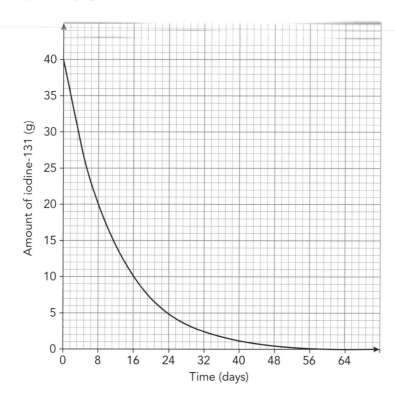

Figure 8.5: Graph showing the radioactive decay of iodine-131

Half-life of iodine-131 = ...

Practice

5   A radioactive substance has a half-life of 13 years.

Calculate the time it will take for the number of undecayed atoms in a sample to fall to one-eighth of the original number.

....

....

6   A scientist measures the activity of a radioactive source as 600 counts per second. Twenty-four hours later she measures the activity again and finds it has dropped to 75 counts per second.

Use this information to determine the half-life of the source.

....

....

7   The table shows how the activity of a radioactive sample changed as it decayed.

Time/h	0	2	4	6	8
Activity/counts per second	500	280	160	95	55

Table 8.5

a   On the graph grid below, draw a graph of activity against time.

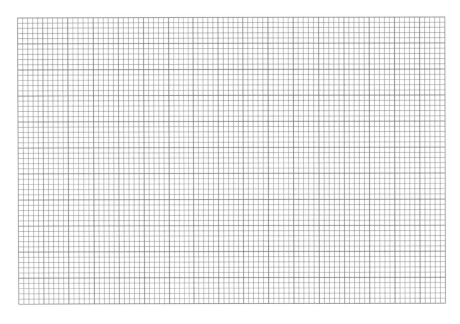

b   Use your graph to deduce the half-life of the substance. Show your method on the graph.

The half-life is approximately ....

Challenge

8   Describe how you could check the value of the half-life you found in question 7. Show your working on the graph.

....

....

....

....

9   A source contains two different elements with unstable nuclei. Isotope A has a
    half-life of 16 hours. Isotope B has a half-life of 8 hours. The count rate from each
    is 128 per second to begin with. Calculate the count rate after 32 hours.

....

....

....

....

Exercise 8.6

IN THIS EXERCISE YOU WILL:

•   practise your understanding of the applications of radioactive isotopes in
    the real world.

Focus

1   A scientist needs to store three radioactive isotopes. She has three containers
    made of different materials – plastic, aluminium and a lead-lined wooden box.
    In the table, identify the correct storage for each isotope.

Isotope	Radiation given out	Container (plastic, aluminium or lead)
A	alpha and gamma	
B	alpha	
C	beta	

Table 8.6

2   Table 8.7 shows some applications of radioactive isotopes. For each application, identify the type of radiation which is used. Then describe the property which makes it suitable for this use.

Use	Alpha, beta or gamma?	Property of radiation which makes it suitable
sterilising medical equipment		
smoke detector		
thickness control in an aluminium foil factory		

Table 8.7

Practice

3   Ionising radiation is dangerous to living things. List and explain the precautions that can be taken to reduce the danger in the following situations:

  a   medical staff using X-rays and gamma rays

  ....

  ....

  b   teachers using radioactive sources to demonstrate radioactivity to students.

  ....

  ....

  ....

4   Ionising radiation can cause mutations that kill cells or lead to cancer. However, ionising radiation can be used in the treatment of cancer. Explain why dangerous radiation can be used as a treatment.

  ....

  ....

  ....

> **TIP**

It is important to understand the difference between contaminated and irradiated.

Soft fruit is often irradiated to give it a longer shelf life. It is safe to eat. Ionising radiation has passed through it, killing bacteria.

Contamination is very different. If the fruit was contaminated, it would have a source of ionising radiation in it or on it. Eating this could be very dangerous indeed, as the source would then be inside you, ionising living tissue.

Challenge

5   Look at the radioisotopes in Table 8.8. Identify the most appropriate radioisotope
    to use for each of these applications. Explain your choice in each case.

a   a medical tracer

....

....

b   to check the thickness of paper in a mill

....

....

c   in a domestic smoke detector

....

....

d   to treat cancer by radiotherapy.

....

....

Radioisotope	Emits	Half-life
Tc-99	gamma	6 hours
Ba-133	gamma	10.5 years
Kr-85	beta, gamma	10.8 years
Am-241	alpha, gamma	432 years
Cf-252	alpha, gamma	2.6 years
La-140	beta, gamma	40.2 hours
U-234	alpha, gamma	250 000 years
I-129	beta, gamma	1 600 000 years

Table 8.8

6 Gamma radiation is the most dangerous form of radiation to be exposed to from outside the body. However, alpha is the most hazardous if it is ingested, for example in food.

Explain why alpha is relatively safe when outside the body, but extremely hazardous if it enters the body.

....

....

....

....

PEER ASSESSMENT

Make a set of flash cards or a mind map to summarise the key facts in this chapter. Highlight key words and definitions you need to learn.

Once you have made a set or cards or your mind map, swap this with someone else and review each other's work.

Having reviewed your partner's work, how can you improve your own work?

Chapter 9

Space physics

> The Solar System

Exercise 9.1

IN THIS EXERCISE YOU WILL:
• check your understanding of the Solar System.

Focus

1   Name the planets in the Solar System, in order of their distance from the Sun.

....

....

Practice

2   The ancient Greek astronomer Ptolemy suggested the model of the Solar System shown in Figure 9.1.

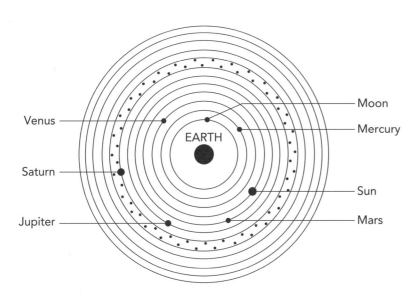

Figure 9.1: Ptolemy's model of the Solar System.

a Describe one way in which Ptolemy's model is different from the model we use now.

....

....

b Describe one way in which Ptolemy's model is similar to the model we use now.

....

....

3 Name the force which keeps the planets in orbit around the Sun.

....

....

....

....

4 Fill in the blanks in the paragraph below.

There are three types of celestial body that orbit the Sun.

These are _____, _____ and _____.

Moons orbit _____.

The Sun is mainly made up of the gases _____ and

_____.

Challenge

5 In 2006, an object which was previously considered to be a planet was reclassified. Use the internet or library books to find the answers to these questions.

a State the name of this object.

....

b State where it is in the Solar System.

....

c Explain why it was reclassified.

....

d State what type of object it is now classified as.

....

6 A learner looks at the data in this table and concludes that:

The larger a planet, the bigger the gravity will be on the surface.

	Mercury	Venus	Earth	Mars	Jupiter	Saturn	Uranus	Neptune
Diameter/km	4879	12104	12756	6792	142984	120536	51118	2370
Mass/10^{24} kg	0.330	4.87	5.97	0.642	1898	568	86.8	0.0146
Gravity/m/s^2	3.7	8.9	9.8	3.7	23.1	9.0	8.7	0.7
Average distance from Sun/10^6 km	57.9	108.2	149.6	227.9	778.6	1433.5	2872.5	5906.4
Orbital period/days	88.0	224.7	365.2	687.0	4331	10747	30589	90560
Mean temperature/°C	167	464	15	−65	−110	−140	−195	−225

Table 9.1

Discuss whether the learner's conclusion is valid. Use the data from the table to support your argument.

....

....

....

> The Sun as a star

Exercise 9.2

IN THIS EXERCISE YOU WILL:

- calculate distances in space

- use light years as a unit of distance.

KEY WORDS

light-year: the distance travelled by light in one year.

> **KEY EQUATION**
>
> $$\text{average orbital speed} = \frac{2 \times \pi \times \text{average radius of orbit}}{\text{time}}$$
>
> $$v = \frac{2\pi r}{T}$$

Focus

1 The Moon is 384 400 km from the Earth. Calculate the time taken for light to travel from the Moon to the Earth. The speed of light is 3×10^8 m/s.

....

....

2 Light from the Sun takes approximately 8.3 minutes to reach the Earth. Calculate the approximate distance from the Sun to the Earth. Give your answer in kilometres.

....

....

Practice

3 a What is a light-year a measure of?

....

b Sirius is the brightest star in our sky. It is 8.6 light-years from Earth. Calculate how far this is in km.

....

c Proxima Centauri is 4.03×10^{13} km away from Earth. Calculate how far this is in light-years.

....

Challenge

4 The Earth orbits the Sun at an average distance of 1.5×10^8 km. The period of its orbit in 365 days.

Calculate the average orbital speed of the Earth around the Sun.

....

5 The Hubble telescope (Figure 9.2) orbits the Earth in a circular orbit.

Figure 9.2: The Hubble telescope.

a Name the force which keeps the Hubble telescope in orbit.

....

b The Hubble telescope orbits 560 km above the surface of the Earth. The Earth has a radius of 6370 km. Calculate the radius of the telescope's orbit.

....

c The time taken for the Hubble telescope to orbit the Earth is 96 minutes. Calculate the orbital speed of the telescope.

....

....

....

Exercise 9.3

IN THIS EXERCISE YOU WILL:

- describe the composition of the Sun

- describe how the Sun affects the movement of the planets.

Focus

1 Name the two gases which our Sun is mainly made up of.

....

2 The Sun radiates energy as electromagnetic waves. Circle the three types of electromagnetic wave which make up most of the Sun's radiation.

   radio waves   **microwaves**   **infrared**   **visible light**

        ultraviolet   **X-rays**   **gamma rays**

Practice

3 Describe the process by which energy is released in stars.

....

....

....

Challenge

4 The Sun's mass makes up about 99.8% of the mass of the Solar System. Describe how this fact helps to explain the movement of the planets.

....

....

5 State how the following change as you get further from the Sun:

   a   the strength of the Sun's gravitational field

   ....

   b   the orbital speed of the planets.

   ....

> The life cycle of stars
Exercise 9.4

IN THIS EXERCISE YOU WILL:

- describe how a star forms
- describe what happens to stars of different masses at the end of their lives.

TIP

All stars start life in the same way. However, what happens after the stable phase depends on mass. More mass means more extreme events and conclusions – supernovae leading to neutron stars and black holes. The more massive a star, the bigger the forces acting inside it, so the more dense the core will be. This is why the biggest stars end up as black holes – so dense that even light cannot escape the pull of their gravity.

Focus

1   Circle the stages which occur in the life cycle of a star similar to our Sun.

   black hole   **protostar**   **red supergiant**   **neutron star**

   white dwarf   **supernova**   **planetary nebula**   **red giant**

2   Circle the stages which may occur in the life cycle of a star which is much more massive than our Sun.

   black hole   **protostar**   **red supergiant**   **red giant**

   neutron star   **white dwarf**   **supernova**   **planetary nebula**

Practice

3   State, in order, the stages our Sun will go through when it reaches the end of its stable period.

   ....

   ....

   ....

KEY WORDS

black hole: the final stage in the life cycle of a star that started with more than eight solar masses; after exploding as a supernova, it still has enough mass to collapse to a point where gravity is so strong that not even light can escape.

interstellar cloud: a cloud of gas and dust that occupies the space between stars.

neutron star: a collapsed star composed almost entirely of neutrons; formed when a star with more than eight solar masses reaches the end of its life.

planetary nebula: a bubble of gas surrounding a white dwarf star that used to be the outer shell of a red giant from which it collapsed.

protostar: a very young star that is still gathering mass from its parent molecular cloud.

4 Describe as fully as possible the life cycle of a star which ends up as a black hole.

....

....

....

....

....

Challenge

5 Explain how a supernova explosion is involved in the formation of new stars.

....

....

6 Canis Major Dwarf is the nearest galaxy to ours. Describe and explain the challenge we face in getting to this galaxy.

....

....

....

KEY WORDS

red giant: a star that began with fewer than eight solar masses and is burning helium in its core; its shell of hydrogen has expanded and cooled.

red supergiant: similar to a red giant; formed when a star with at least eight times the mass of the Sun runs out of hydrogen fuel in its core but fusion of hydrogen continues in the outer shells.

stable star: a star that is not collapsing or expanding; the inward force of gravity is balanced by radiation pressure, which pushes outwards.

supernova: an exploding star that began life with more than eight solar masses and has run out of fuel.

white dwarf: the final stage of a star that started with fewer than eight solar masses after all its fuel has been used up.

> Galaxies and the Universe

Exercise 9.5

IN THIS EXERCISE YOU WILL:

- describe the make-up of the Universe and how it was formed.

TIP

Distances in space are difficult to imagine. It is worth spending some time thinking about them.

We think of travelling to the Moon as a long journey but it takes light only 1.3 seconds to reach us from the Moon.

Light from the Sun takes about 8 minutes to reach us, while light from Proxima Centauri takes 4.2 light-years.

The diameter of the Milky Way is 100 000 light-years and astronomers in 2022 measured light from a distant galaxy which is 13.5 billion light-years away!

Focus

1 Figure 9.3 shows the Milky Way.

Figure 9.3: The Milky Way.

a State what the Milky Way is.

....

b Circle the best description of the number of stars in the Milky Way.

   thousands   **millions**   **billions**

c Circle the best description of the number of galaxies in the Universe.

   thousands   **millions**   **billions**

Practice

2   List the following structures in order of size.

        universe   **star**   **planet**   **galaxy**

   ....

3   State the diameter of the Milky Way galaxy in light-years. ....

4   Write the following distances in order, with the shortest first.
   A   The distance from the Sun to the nearest stars in the Milky Way galaxy
   B   The distance from the Moon to the Earth
   C   The distance from the Earth to the Sun
   D   The distance from the Earth to Mars.

   ....

Challenge

5   The Big Bang theory explains many observations made by astronomers.

   State *three* things that the theory tells us about the Universe.

   ....

   ....

   ....

6   Proxima Centauri is about 4.35 light-years from Earth. It has a planet called
   Proxima Centauri b which scientists believe may be habitable. Explain why it is not
   feasible to send a probe to explore Proxima Centauri b as we have done with Mars.

   ....

   ....

   ....

PEER ASSESSMENT

Make a mind map to summarise the key facts in this chapter. Once you have
made it, swap it with someone else and review each other's work. Can you
make any improvements to your mind map?

> Glossary

acceleration: the rate of change of an object's velocity.

a.c. generator: a device, such as a dynamo, used to generate alternating current (a.c.).

alpha decay: the decay of a radioactive nucleus by emission of an alpha particle; the general equation for this decay is $^A_Z X = ^{A-4}_{Z-2} Y + ^4_2 \alpha$.

alpha particle (α-particle): a particle of two protons and two neutrons emitted by an atomic nucleus during radioactive decay.

ammeter: a meter for measuring electric current.

amp, ampere (A): the SI unit of electric current.

amplitude: the greatest height of a wave above its undisturbed level.

angle of incidence: the angle between the incident ray and the normal.

angle of reflection: the angle between the reflected ray and the normal.

angle of refraction: the angle between the refracted ray and the normal.

asteroids: lumps of rock that orbit the Sun.

background radiation: the nuclear radiation from the environment to which we are exposed all the time, due to the disintegration of unstable nuclei.

battery: two or more electrical cells connected together in series; the word may also be used to mean a single cell.

beta decay: the decay of a radioactive nucleus by emission of a beta particle.

beta particle (β-particle): an electron emitted by a nucleus during radioactive decay.

biomass fuel: a material, recently living, used as a fuel.

black hole: the final stage in the life cycle of a star that started with more than eight solar masses; after exploding as a supernova, it still has enough mass to collapse to a point where gravity is so strong that not even light can escape.

Brownian motion: the motion of microscopic particles suspended in a liquid or gas, caused by molecular bombardment.

cell: a device that provides an electromotive force (voltage) in a circuit by means of a chemical reaction.

centre of gravity: the point at which the mass of an object can be considered to be concentrated.

chemical potential energy: energy stored in chemical substances and which can be released in a chemical reaction.

commutator: a device used to allow current to flow to and from the coil of a d.c. motor or generator.

conduction: the transfer of thermal energy or electricity through a material without movement of the material itself.

conductor: a substance that allows an electric current to pass through it or a substance that transmits thermal energy.

convection: the transfer of thermal energy through a material by movement of the material itself.

converging lens: rays that enter a converging lens parallel to the principal axis pass through the principal focus after leaving the lens; these lenses usually form real images.

coulomb (C): the SI unit of electric charge.

count rate: the number of nuclear disintegrations per second; measured in counts/min or counts/s.

crest/peak: the highest point of a wave.

critical angle: the minimum angle of incidence at which total internal reflection occurs; it has the symbol c.

current: a flow of electric charge; the charge passing a point in a circuit per second.

deceleration: negative acceleration (the rate of decrease of velocity).

density: the ratio of mass to volume for a substance.

diffraction: the spreading out of a wave as it passes through a gap.

doing work: transferring energy.

efficiency: the fraction of energy that is transferred to a useful form.

elastic (strain) energy: energy stored in the changed shape of an object.

electric field: a region where charged objects experience a force; the direction of the field at a point in the field is the direction of force on a positive charge at that point.

electromagnet: a coil of wire that becomes a magnet when a current flows in it. An electromagnet can be turned on or off. The strength of an electromagnet depends on the size of the current flowing through the coil of wire (the solenoid).

electromagnetic induction: the process by which a potential difference is induced across a conductor when the magnetic field around it changes.

electromagnetic radiation: energy travelling in the form of waves.

electromagnetic spectrum: a range of electromagnetic waves with different wavelengths, which travel at the same speed (the speed of light) and can travel through a vacuum.

electromotive force (e.m.f): the voltage across a cell or power supply.

electron: a negatively-charged particle, smaller than an atom.

electrostatic charge: a property of an object that causes it to attract or repel other objects with charge.

energy: quantity that must be changed or transferred to make something happen; the capacity to do work.

equilibrium: when no net force and no net moment act on a body.

extension: the increase in length of an object (for example, a spring) when a load (for example, a weight) is attached to it.

Fleming's left-hand rule: a rule that shows the relative directions of force, magnetic field and current when a current-carrying conductor is placed in a magnetic field.

focal length: the distance between the centre of a lens and the principal focus.

force: the action of one body on a second body that causes its velocity to change.

fossil fuel: a material formed from long-dead material, used as a fuel.

frequency: the number of vibrations per second or the number of waves per second passing a point.

fuse: a device used to prevent excessive currents flowing in a circuit.

gamma ray (γ-ray): electromagnetic radiation emitted by an atomic nucleus during radioactive decay.

geothermal: the energy stored in hot rocks underground.

gravitational potential energy: energy stored in an object that is raised up against the force of gravity.

half-life: the average time taken for half the atoms in a sample of a radioactive material to decay.

hard magnetic material: a material that, once magnetised, is difficult to demagnetise; steel is a hard magnetic material.

Hertz: the unit of frequency; 1 Hz = 1 wave per second.

infrared radiation: electromagnetic radiation whose wavelength is greater than that of visible light; sometimes known as thermal radiation.

insulator: a substance that does not conduct electricity or a substance that transmits thermal energy very poorly.

internal energy: the energy of an object; the total kinetic and potential energies of its particles.

interstellar cloud: a cloud of gas and dust that occupies the space between stars.

ionising radiation: radiation, for example from radioactive substances, that causes ionisation.

isotope: isotopes of an element have the same proton number but different nucleon numbers.

joule (J): the SI unit of work or energy.

kinetic energy: energy stored in a moving object.

kinetic particle model of matter: a model in which matter consists of molecules in motion.

light-year: the distance travelled by light in one year.

limit of proportionality: up to this limit, the extension on a spring is proportional to load.

load: the force (usually weight) that stretches an object (a spring).

longitudinal wave: a wave in which the vibration is forward and back, along the direction in which the wave is travelling.

magnet: a device which exerts a force on magnetic materials.

magnetic field: the region of space around a magnet or electric current in which a magnet will feel a force.

magnetic field line: a line showing the force exerted by a magnetic field; the direction of a magnetic field line at a point in a magnetic field is the direction of the force on a North pole placed at that point.

magnetic material: a material on which a magnet exerts a force and which can be magnetised; common magnetic materials are iron, steel, nickel, cobalt.

magnetisation: causing a piece of material to be magnetised; a material is magnetised when it produces a magnetic field around itself.

mass: a measure of the quantity of matter in an object at rest relative to the observer.

minor planet: an object which orbits the Sun but is too small or too close to another object to be defined as a planet.

moment of a force: the turning effect of a force about a point.

negative charge: one of the two types of electric charge; the other is positive charge.

neutral: having no overall positive or negative electric charge.

neutron: an electrically neutral particle found in the atomic nucleus.

neutron number (N): the number of neutrons in an atomic nucleus.

neutron star: a collapsed star composed almost entirely of neutrons; formed when a star with more than eight solar masses reaches the end of its life.

non-renewable: energy resource which, once used, is gone forever.

normal: 'at 90°'; a normal is a line at 90° to a surface (for example, the surface of a mirror) or boundary between two materials (for example, the boundary between air and glass).

nuclear fission: the process by which energy is released by the splitting of a large heavy nucleus into two or more lighter nuclei.

nuclear fusion: the process by which energy is released by the joining together of two small light nuclei to form a new heavier nucleus.

nuclear potential energy: energy stored in the nucleus of an atom.

nucleon: a particle found in the atomic nucleus – a proton or a neutron.

nucleon number (A): the number of protons and neutrons in an atomic nucleus.

nuclide: a 'species' of nucleus having particular values of proton number and nucleon number.

ohm (Ω): the SI unit of electrical resistance.

orbit: the path of an object as it moves around a larger object.

parallel circuit: a circuit in which there is more than one path which the current can take.

p.d. (potential difference): another name for the voltage between two points.

penetration: how far radiation can travel into different materials.

period: the time for one complete vibration or the passage of one complete wave.

pitch: how high or low a note sounds.

plane (mirror): plane means 'flat', so a plane mirror is a flat mirror.

planet: a large spherical object that orbits the Sun without another similar object close to it.

planetary nebula: a bubble of gas surrounding a white dwarf star that used to be the outer shell of a red giant from which it collapsed.

positive charge: one of the two types of electric charge; the other is negative charge.

power: the rate at which work is done or energy is transferred.

power lines: cables used to carry electricity from power stations to consumers.

pressure: the force acting per unit area at right angles to a surface.

principal axis: the line passing through the centre of a lens, perpendicular to its surface.

principal focus: the point at which rays of light parallel to the principal axis converge after passing through a converging lens.

principle of conservation of energy: the total energy of interacting objects is constant provided no net external force acts.

proton: a positively-charged particle found in the atomic nucleus.

proton number (Z): the number of protons in an atomic nucleus.

protostar: a very young star that is still gathering mass from its parent molecular cloud.

radiation: energy spreading out from a source carried by particles or waves.

radioactive decay: the disintegration of the nucleus of a radioactive substance, when its nuclei emit radiation.

radioactive substance: a substance that decays by emitting radiation from its atomic nuclei.

random process: a process that happens at a random rate rather than at a steady rate; in radioactive decay, it is impossible to predict which atom will decay next, or when a given atom will decay.

ray diagram: a diagram showing the paths of typical rays of light.

real image: an image that can be formed on a screen.

red giant: a star that began with fewer than eight solar masses and is burning helium in its core; its shell of hydrogen has expanded and cooled.

red supergiant: similar to a red giant; formed when a star with at least eight times the mass of the Sun runs out of hydrogen fuel in its core but fusion of hydrogen continues in the outer shells.

reflection: the change in direction of a ray of light or a wave when it strikes a surface without passing through it.

refraction: the bending of a ray of light or a wave on passing from one material to another.

refractive index: the ratio of the speeds of a wave in two different regions.

renewable: energy resource which, when used, will be replenished naturally.

resistance: the ratio of the p.d. across a component to the current flowing through it.

resistor: a component in an electric circuit which limits or controls the flow of current.

resultant force: the single force that has the same effect on a body as two or more forces.

right-hand grip rule: the rule used to determine the direction of the magnetic field around a wire carrying an electric current.

series circuit: a circuit in which there is only one path the current can take around the circuit.

slip rings: a component used to allow current to flow to and from the coil of an a.c. motor or generator.

soft magnetic material: a material that, once magnetised, is easily demagnetised; soft iron is a soft magnetic material.

solenoid: a long narrow coil of wire.

spectrum: waves, or colours of light, separated out in order according to their wavelengths.

speed: the distance travelled by an object in unit time.

speed of light: the speed at which light travels; this is 3.0×10^8 m/s in a vacuum.

spring constant: the constant of proportionality; the measure of the stiffness of a spring.

stable star: a star that is not collapsing or expanding; the inward force of gravity is balanced by radiation pressure, which pushes outwards.

supernova: an exploding star that began life with more than eight solar masses and has run out of fuel.

thermal energy: energy transferred from a hotter place to a colder place because of the temperature difference between them.

thermal expansion: the expansion of a material when its temperature rises.

total internal reflection: when a ray of light strikes the inner surface of a solid material and 100% of the light reflects back inside the material.

transformer: a device used to change the voltage of an a.c. electricity supply.

transverse wave: a wave in which the vibration is at right angles to the direction in which the wave is travelling.

trip switch: a safety device that automatically switches off a circuit when the current becomes too high.

trough: the lowest point of a wave.

ultraviolet radiation: electromagnetic radiation whose frequency is higher than that of visible light.

variable resistor: a resistor whose resistance can be changed, for example by turning a knob.

velocity: speed in a given direction.

virtual image: an image that cannot be formed on a screen; it is formed when rays of light appear to be spreading out from a point.

volt (V): the SI unit of voltage (p.d. or e.m.f.).

voltage: the 'push' of a battery or power supply in a circuit.

voltmeter: a meter for measuring voltage or potential difference.

watt (W): the SI unit of power; the power when 1 J of work is done in 1 s; 1 W = 1 J/s.

wavelength: the distance between adjacent crests (or troughs) of a wave.

wave speed: the speed at which a wave travels.

weight: the downward force of gravity that acts on an object because of its mass.

white dwarf: the final stage of a star that started with fewer than eight solar masses after all its fuel has been used up.

work done: the amount of energy transferred.

> Acknowledgements

The authors and publishers acknowledge the following sources of copyright material and are grateful for the permissions granted. While every effort has been made, it has not always been possible to identify the sources of all the material used, or to trace all copyright holders. If any omissions are brought to our notice, we will be happy to include the appropriate acknowledgements on reprinting.

Thanks to the following for permission to reproduce images:

Cover Sebastien GABORIT/GI; Figure 1.8 Avalon_Studio/GI; Figure 1.10 Wong Sze Fei/GI; Figure 1.20 Thomas Northcut/GI; Figure 2.8 Tom Merton/GI; Figure 3.5 Andrew Lambert Photography/SCIENCE PHOTO LIBRARY; Figure 3.8 Bill Oxford/GI; Figure 6.14 mikroman6/GI; Figure 9.2 Stocktrek Images/ GI; Figure 9.3 Mark Garlick/Science Photo Library/GI

GI = Getty Images